D0804212

the Marked Bible

Charles L. Taylor

Pacific Press® Publishing Association
Nampa, Idaho
Oshawa, Ontario, Canada

Designed by Ira Lee
Cover by Duane Tank

Printed in the United States of America

ISBN 0-8163-0803-9

04 • 24

INTRODUCTION

The author of this book was pre-eminently a soul winner and builder. He gave his heart to God at the early age of fifteen, and two years later dedicated his all to his chosen Master's service. Educational work was part of his life. He taught in schools in California, Georgia, Washington, Minnesota, Ohio, and Michigan, closing his teaching work in a college in Michigan. His experience as a chaplain for years in a large sanitarium brought him into close and intimate touch with the sick and suffering.

He had an exceptional gift as a clear, convincing writer, a spirit and style peculiarly impressive and sympathetic. His great desire was to present Biblical truth with a new luster that would guide men to heaven.

There is not a phase of life presented in this booklet, not an inconsistent argument against the truth of God, that has not been witnessed over and over.

The circulation of *The Marked Bible* exceeds two million copies. The book has been translated into many languages. Of the author it may be said:

> He saw God's truth, but did not stay
> To ask if others saw the way.
> Content was he in heart to know
> That Jesus walked there, here below.
> And evermore He walks with men,
> That men may walk His paths again.
> And He is more than all besides;
> For others fail, but He abides.

THE PUBLISHERS.

CHAPTER I

A Rebellious Son: A Mother's Love

'DON'T mention it again, I tell you—never again. I am *tired* of all this talk about Christianity, and I'm not going to stand it any longer. You may do as you please, but I insist that you stop making life here at home so unpleasant for me."

"But, son, remember father. His dying request was for you. Just let me tell you of one thing he said about you in his last prayer. He called me to his bedside, and with choked voice—"

"Mother, you seem to think I don't mean what I say, and so you *will* keep on. But I have my mind made up to end this whole business. I may as well tell you that one week from today I am going to sea. Now please let me live in peace the few days I am here with you, and I will be thankful."

Mrs. Wilson had been a wise, tactful mother. For fifteen long years she had been alone in the world, battling with poverty, but always seeking faithfully to shield her child from the corrupting influence of the great city in which she had her home.

It was not true, however, that she had been given to much talk, as might be supposed from the son's complaint. As a mother ought, she had wisely restrained him, and had insisted that her decisions be respected. But her words had been few, especially during recent years, when Harold's age demanded that he begin to fulfill the responsibilities of manhood, and to act more fully the independent part of life.

When his father died, Harold was a boy of eight years. From his birth, he had been dedicated to God. It was the supreme ambition of both father and mother that he should be trained for the work of the gospel. They wanted him to devote his life to proclaiming the good news of Him who died to save from sin, and who would one day come again in glory to receive His people to Himself. Theirs was a "blessed hope," and their child gave promise of reaching the end they sought. He was a handsome boy, and early gave evidence of a love for the things of God.

Then a change came. The kind and careful husband and father was stricken down with a fatal illness. For many months he lay ill, and the means he had been saving up for his boy's education were taken for the payment of the ever-increasing bills. Finally all the money was gone. When at last the end was in sight, he called his wife and son to his side, and together they prayed once more that God would remember the consecration they had made, and in His own good way and time bring little Harold to be a soul winner for Christ, as they had planned.

"Does God hear? *Does* He answer?" These were the questions that had been presenting themselves to Mrs. Wilson's mind for more than two years now. Notwithstanding all her pleadings, all her tears, all her struggles, the influence of worldly associations had gradually and surely alienated her son from God. More and more he had come to manifest a positive dislike for all that pertained to God and His word of truth.

At the time this story opens, Harold had become an alcoholic, a gambler, a thief. He seemed the exact reproduction, in his characteristics, of a great-grandfather whose life had been made notorious by atheism, blasphemy, drunkenness, and murder, and who had ended his life on the gallows. As Mrs. Wilson thought upon this fact,—that in her son was being fulfilled the scripture, "Visiting the iniquity of the fathers upon the children unto the third and fourth generation,"—her heart almost broke within her, and she began to despair.

She had been led to speak to her son once more because of crime recently committed in the neighborhood of her home, and suspicion rested upon him. In her heart she little doubted that he was involved, and the thought so cruelly hurt her that she could not remain silent. Hence she spoke.

But when she did so, there came the last crushing disappointment. She was told never again to mention the subject of a better life. In fact, she was to have slight opportunity, for Harold had declared his intention of going to sea, and only a few days intervened. Besides, he was going under a cloud, very probably to escape the clutches of the law.

"Oh, my boy, my boy! I have prayed and prayed that you might grow to be a noble, God-fearing man. I have asked God continually to take you for His service. I have done all I have known to do to keep you from the world. I have hoped and trusted that you would be kept. But today you are a criminal, a godless, wicked man. You hate religion. You turn from me as though I were one of your worst enemies. Oh, my Harold, my treasure, must I give you up?"

Thus spoke Mrs. Wilson to herself out of the agony of her heart after her son had so ruthlessly denied her the privilege of again speaking to him of the Christian hope.

And while his mother mourned and wept, Harold caroused. With an almost fiendish enthusiasm, he joined with his associates in riotous pleasure, and more than once his voice was heard in denunciation of his parents' hopes. He drank and cursed, and even challenged the Almighty, if He existed, to come and strike him down if He dared. So far had he fallen!

Does God hear? *Does* God answer? *Had* a mother's prayers been unheeded? Had all those years of toil and sacrifice and devotion and trust been in vain?—No, thank God, No.

> Think not, thou mother heart,
>   That God hears not thy cry.
> Thine interests are His,
>   And He is standing nigh.
> He listens, waits, and longs to prove
> That He is God, thy God, thy Love.
>
> Nor doubt, then, nor despair;
>   Trust on through dark, through light;
> Fear not to bide His time;
>   He'll surely do the right.
> He knows the secrets of thy soul.
> Thy son shall one day be made whole.

It was a terribly dark hour to the dear mother; and worn out with the heavy burden, and not seeing as yet the welcome approach of a brighter day, she lay down and fell asleep.

She dreamed!

It was the morning of eternity. The world was new. All marks of the curse were gone. Sin and all its consequences had been removed forever. She saw the Saviour. She saw the saints of all the ages, the innumerable multitudes with the palms and the harps. And ere she could have a moment of disappointment, there stood by her side her companion of early years. He looked into her face, radiant with life; and then, out of the fullness of his supreme joy, he said, "And here is Harold!"

"Yes, here I am, father," came the musical answer of him who had been precious in their eyes; and then he stood before them—their son, made over into the image of the blessed Christ.

"Harold, O Harold! Bless God! My Father *did* hear and He *did* answer. Ah, I thought you would not come! And how did the Master find and redeem you?"

"Mother, do you remember the marked Bible you hid among my things the day I left you and went to sea? The message you wrote in the Book, and the message of the Book itself, broke my hardened spirit, and I could not find rest until I laid my weary self at His feet. He lifted me up, He taught me of the right way, He guided my soul to this better land."

How long she slept, Mrs. Wilson knew not; but when she awoke, it was long past midnight, and she heard Harold stumbling up to his room.

But why did his heavy, uncertain step this time fail to trouble her as it had before? Why could she resign herself to what seemed a veritable tragedy, which was wrecking her home?

She was not a believer in dreams. She did not regard the beautiful picture that had been projected upon the screen of her mind as being necessarily divine. There had come to her, however, in the experience, a suggestion of a new work of love. She had found also a new basis for hope, a new vision of possibilities; and with a mother's loyal quickness, her plans were immediately formulated for putting the suggestion into practice.

What a blessed mission was that of the new day, when with her widow's mite—the savings of many a long, weary day—she found her way to the heart of the city, and there invested that mite in a Bible for Harold! She bought the best that was possible, leaving nothing remaining for the coming "rainy day." Was not her son's life more precious to her than her own?

What a really wonderful Bible that was when Mrs. Wilson had completed in it her beautiful design! From Genesis to Revelation she marked, with great care, those passages which she believed would one day appeal to the heart of her boy. Just what texts and just what markings entered into the plan may not be told here; suffice it to say that only a wise, loving, praying mother could ever have thought out and executed so splendid a soul-winning idea.

Without doing violence to the sacredness of a mother's secret, it may be stated that two great principles were emphasized—faith in Jesus as a complete Saviour, and obedience to *all* His commandments. Mrs. Wilson had learned that Jesus is the only Messiah of the Scriptures; that it was He who created the world; who spoke through prophets; who conversed with patriarchs; who gave the law on Sinai; who led Israel into the Promised Land; who walked and talked with Adam, with Enoch, with Noah, with Abraham, with Moses, with David. She understood that He was "the Lamb slain from the foundation of the world," and that therefore before the time of Calvary as well as after, men were saved through Him. To her, the whole Bible was a Jesus book, one story of the Friend of sinners.

When Harold should open the Book, she wanted him to find Christ everywhere throughout the story, to hear His voice, to know His love, and then to render Him service.

It was only natural, in view of this, that she made particularly prominent the claims of the Ten Commandments. If Christ had spoken them, and then had *died that they might be written in man's heart,* were they not vital to salvation?

Her own message, written on the flyleaf, and accidentally stained with a tear that fell as she wrote, was this:

"My Darling Boy:

"I love you. I shall *always* love you. But there is One who loves you infinitely more than I, and that One is Jesus. You do not love Him now; but I am praying that you may be brought to see how good He is, and be led to yield yourself to Him. This Book is from Him and from me. *Please read it* for His sake and for mine. Its promises are all sure; and as you take them into your heart, they will make you new and clean and strong and victorious.

"Lovingly,
"Mother."

The marked Bible waited in secret until almost the last moment before Harold's leave-taking; and then, when he was absent on an errand, it was quickly tucked away out of sight in one corner of his box.

"Good-by, mother!"

"Good-by, my dearest," she said; and putting her arms around Harold's neck, she gave him a long farewell embrace. The tears wanted to come; but she had determined on another course, and a smile of peace wreathed her face instead.

CHAPTER II

A Godly Sea Captain's Answered Prayer

IT WAS a bright May morning when the "Alaska Transport" with Harold Wilson aboard as an ordinary deck hand, put out through the Golden Gate for Melbourne. It was a day of gloom to Harold. Notwithstanding the apparent bravado of his hardened life, down deep in his heart there was a something akin to boyhood tenderness which he could not throw aside.

As the great vessel, responding to her mighty propeller, gained in momentum and was quickly finding her way out into the great Pacific, and the shores of the homeland began to fade from view, there came to Harold, for the first time in many years, a partial consciousness of the value of a mother. He could not explain why; but now that she was no longer within reach, no longer where he could realize her presence, she began to assume a different appearance to his mind's eye. After all, she was beautiful; and could he have made the wake of the vessel a path for returning, he would gladly have hastened home.

Of course, this feeling was only temporary; yet it showed that the time was not altogether past when a mother's love appealed to this son's affections. And it was this tender spot which a great Providence was to touch, and through which it would work to cause Harold Wilson to forsake his sins.

The tear that stole its way to the young man's cheek was quickly brushed away, and he resolutely strove to drown all thought of a mother's prayers and the purpose for which they were offered. He said to himself, "Be game, old man, and don't play the baby!" And surely he seemed to succeed in his determination to forget.

The crew of the "Alaska Transport" was the usual motley group of different nationalities, nearly all of whom were abandoned to drink, profanity, and irreligion. Among them, Harold was a "hail fellow well met."

"Hello! What's this?" Harold was in search of a needed garment; and as he pulled it from his sailor's chest, a package fell to the floor.

"I never saw this before," he exclaimed, and hastily removed the wrapper.

"A Bible! A Bible! And did mother think me such an idiot that I would stand for such nonsense? But, say, it's a dandy book. I wonder what it cost. My! but this is funny! Harold Wilson, a common drunk, and a thief besides, having a Bible at sea! I guess I'll ask for the job of preaching to the boys."

He opened the Book, "just to see how a Bible looks inside;" and there, in the familiar writing of his good mother, were the words, "My Darling Boy." A lump came into his throat. For an instant he was transported back to his childhood, and he saw himself in his innocence, enjoying the endearing words which for so long a time now he had professed to spurn. Again a tear, an unwelcome tear, made its way down his cheek. Instinctively he turned his face, lest the eye of some fellow sailor should discover his weakness.

But he could not resist reading his mother's brief message written on the flyleaf. Nor did he lay the Book down—rather, throw it down—until he had glanced through its pages, and discovered the markings of his tender mother's hand. Not only were passages marked, but in connection, written in the margin, were words of truth and admonition which only his mother could ever have penned.

"I don't want this thing," he cried out. "Must I be haunted by this miserable stuff wherever I go?" and throwing the Book into the box, he slammed down the cover, and "turned in" for the night.

About a month had passed, and a hard month indeed it had been. The journey had been made through rough seas, and on more than one occasion there had been imminent danger. And then a fire broke out in the hold.

The "Alaska Transport" had aboard a heavy consignment of kerosene oil, and a fire meant almost certain death to all on board. A strong force of fire fighters was therefore set to work in a frantic effort to smother the flames before they should reach the cargo of oil.

Captain Mann, who was in charge of the vessel, was a Christian, a person of few words, and a man whose personality commanded the respect and even the admiration of his men. He was courteous, brave, temperate, refined, a striking exception to the rank and file of the crew that manned the ship. For more than thirty years he had been in command at sea; but this was his first experience with a burning vessel.

The cry of "Fire!" had called forth the strongest that was in him. Though his nature almost staggered at the peril of the situation, he calmly but quickly placed every man at his post; and every man fought with confidence because of something that Captain Mann possessed in this period of danger. Harold Wilson in particular took note of the spirit of courage and confidence shown by him.

But suddenly the captain disappeared. And almost as suddenly, a new emergency compelled the first mate to call for his assistance. Harold Wilson was dispatched to find him.

Pale with fear, the young man hastened to the captain's room. The door stood ajar. He was about to call out his message when a voice from within checked him.

It was the voice of prayer!

To make certain, he pushed the door a bit farther open, and, lo, there was the captain on his knees, his Bible open before him, his face turned upward.

The throbbing of the engines and the general excitement aboard had caused Harold's coming to be unnoticed; and thus the captain continued his prayer, while Harold seemed spellbound.

The prayer touched a responsive chord. Why should it not? It was a prayer that the God of the Bible would fulfill His promise, and save the lives of the crew; and Harold Wilson was one whose life was in the balance. For the first time in his career, he was glad to see a praying man.

Captain Mann's Bible refuge was Psalm 107:23-31. This assurance was his comfort now. Whether storm or fire, it mattered not; God would bring them "out of their distresses," "unto their desired haven." This was the promise which Harold Wilson heard Captain Mann plead.

But strange to say, Psalm 107:23-31 was one of the

passages Mrs. Wilson had marked in the Bible given her son.

Was the captain's prayer to be answered?

Harold had only a moment to wait, for Captain Mann was soon on his feet and hastening back to his perilous duty. Harold made known his message, and also rushed again to his post.

The fire had been gaining headway rapidly, despite heroic resistance. The vessel seemed doomed. In a few minutes, the vast cargo of oil must ignite, and then all would be over.

But now a great explosion took place. The closed hatches were almost blown from the deck. The crew were terror-stricken, not knowing but that the oil was already in the grip of the fire.

What had happened?—Ah, one of those providential things which only the Christian can understand. A large steam pipe had burst and was now pouring an immense volume of superheated steam and water into the hold at the point of greatest danger. An unseen hand had assumed control. Soon the volumes of black smoke gave place to clouds of white steam, and the fighters knew that the salvation of the ship was assured.

So wonderful did it all seem, the crew were not slow to express their astonishment and gratitude.

"Do yez belave, captain, that the Big Mon had somethin' to do with it?" inquired a rough Irishman, Pat Moran by name.

Captain Mann had perhaps erred in his views regarding religious life in one respect. He held it unnecessary to talk to his men about Christianity, but rather allowed them to discover what they could about his ideas from what he actually lived before them.

But now he was drawn out to confess his faith.

"Men," said he, "that steam pipe was broken by the hand of the Almighty. It did not merely 'happen.' There is a God who hears and answers prayer. He has promised to help men who go to sea, and today He has kept His word."

Harold's marked Bible, like an unwelcome spirit, seemed to haunt him as he listened.

"But say, captain, do yez railly belave what yer sayin'?" again spoke Pat.

"Ah, my boy, I have believed for many long years."

"But where did yez get the idee? Where has the Big Mon told yez that He would take care of us poor lunatics?"

"Pat, I had a good mother, who taught me to pray to God up in heaven. She taught me, also, to read the Bible, the Book that God helped good men to write. In that Book, He tells us that we all belong to Him, that we are to obey Him, and that He will take care of us. He says He will save men who are in trouble while traveling the seas. Did you never see a Bible, Pat?"

"Shure, an' I niver did," he exclaimed; "but, belave me, I would like to put the eye of me on such a wurruk."

Again Harold Wilson was ill at ease. A good mother, a God, a Bible, an answered prayer—all these thoughts were as goads, which hurt, and hurt deeply. Had he not a good mother? Had she not taught him to believe in God and to pray? Had she not often appealed to him to read the Bible and to obey its precepts?—Yes, all this and much more.

Pat Moran, and others at this time off duty, accepted Captain Mann's invitation to go to his room and look at the promise which that day had saved the lives of all on board. Harold went with them.

The Bible lay open on the table near the door.

"There, men, is the Book my mother taught me to love," said the captain; "and right there is the promise which put out the fire and saved your lives and mine." He read to them, as he spoke, the scripture which for a long time had been his refuge.

Harold looked into the captain's face. What a good face! How clean looking, and how free from coarseness! Honesty, sincerity, nobility, were to be traced in every furrow. And this was a man of the Bible, a practical, helpful, wholehearted sea captain.

Quickly filling his mouth with a chew of plug tobacco, Harold hastened from the room to his own part of the vessel. Nervously throwing open his box, he snatched up the Bible given him by his mother, and tried to find the verses that the captain had just read. He finally found them.

In the margin, he read these words from his mother's pen: "I shall ever pray that this promise may be your refuge at sea, to save you from storm or accident."

He closed the Book, and angrily threw it down— angry to think that he had not succeeded in getting beyond the reach of his mother's influence. The entire experience was like a nightmare.

No sooner, therefore, did he see this text and its accompanying statement, than he felt within him all the old-time antagonism and bitterness. Giving way to all his pent-up wrath, he sprang to his feet with a curse on his lips. He took the Bible to the open door and impetuously threw it far out into the sea.

"There, that ends this whole cursed business," he muttered; and then, imagining that he had performed a praiseworthy act, he sauntered out on deck.

CHAPTER III

Sad News From Home

"OH, MOTHER, mother!" Harold Wilson stood in the post office at Honolulu, holding in his hand a letter sent by an old friend in California. It read as follows:

"FRIEND HAROLD:

"We have been hoping for several weeks for your return home. We had heard indirectly that you were on the way home, and we were encouraged to believe you might come in time to be a support to your mother during her last illness.

"Several weeks ago she had a hard fall, superinducing pneumonia. She made a brave fight; but her anxiety over you, coupled with financial reverses, proved too much for her, and she passed away last Thursday.

"Her last request was that I should write to you, and urge you not to forget the gift she placed in your box the day you left home. You will know, of course, to what she referred. She did not tell me its nature, but she did say that it took all she had in the world to get it for you.

"By the way, my boy, since you left us, I have changed

my whole course of life. No more drinking, gambling, or profanity for me. I am a Christian now and am enjoying life wonderfully.

"God bless you! Don't be discouraged over your great loss. Live for Christ, and you will meet her again.

"I am sending this to Honolulu at a venture.

"Your one-time friend in booze, but now free,

"HOWARD HUFFMAN."

Yes, Harold had been working his way homeward. For many years he had been absent, during which time he had seen much of the world, visiting Australia, China, South Africa, South America, and Europe.

He had continued his hard life of drink and profanity, always planning to do better when he saw his mother again. He had thrown overboard his beautiful Bible, in order to silence the voice of the Reprover; but never once had he seen a day of peace. Somehow the heartless ingratitude of that moment when his anger caused him to destroy his mother's gift, had become a nemesis, which seemed to trail his every step and to bring him only defeat and failure in all he undertook.

Honolulu was "almost home" to him, and his heart was already beginning to enjoy a foretaste of the blessed reunion with mother. Like the prodigal of the Scripture, he had formulated his confession; and he was confident that, restored to his mother, he should be able to "make good."

One may easily understand, therefore, what were his feelings as the letter from home was placed in his hands —feelings of deep heart satisfaction.

But how cruel was the disappointment! The words, "She passed away last Thursday," fell upon his soul as a bolt of lightning from out the blue. He was stunned.

"Oh, mother, *mother!*" he cried, forgetting that all around him were strangers, from whom he must hide his grief. And then under his breath he said, "You wanted to help me, you could have helped me; but now you're gone, gone, g-o-n-e."

He picked up the missive, and hurried into the street and down to the launch that was to convey him to his vessel.

"Harold Wilson, what will you do now? Will you be a man, as you ought to be, or will you absolutely and perhaps forever throw yourself away?" Such were the questions that something seemed to whisper in his ear as he boarded the ship, which was to sail next day.

The answer was at once forthcoming; but, sad to say, it was an answer dictated by his lower nature.

As with many others, inability on Harold's part to carry out his plan made him desperate and ofttimes apparently irresponsible. He had been acknowledging the existence of God, and he had planned that when with his mother he would lead a better life. But this thwarting of plans angered him, and he now determined to go deeper into wickedness than ever before.

"There is no God. If there is, He is only a brute, and I hate Him. He hates me, because He robs me of my mother at the very time I need her. Oh, I'll show Him, if He lives, that Harold Wilson can outdo Him. If He won't let me do right, I'll do wrong."

And surely it seemed that from that day forward, he succeeded in fitting his life to his resolution; for upon reaching San Francisco, he abandoned himself to a course of riotous pleasure, licentiousness, and crime. His companions were of the baser elements of the city, versed in the business of lawbreaking, even to the extent of staining their hands with the blood of their fellow men.

Howard Huffman, the writer of the message sent to Honolulu, picked up the morning *Chronicle*. As he glanced over the headings, his eye was held by the following:

"Murder in the Mission District. Harold Wilson a Sailor Held as a Suspect. Police Sure They Have the Right Man, an Old Criminal."

Mr. Huffman paled and dropped his paper. "An old criminal." Yes, he knew it to be true; for in that robbery of many years before, he himself had been associated. And now Harold had returned to continue his course in crime. What should he do?

Fearing to breathe to his young wife the cause of his agitation, he hurriedly donned his coat and hat and left the house.

The Huffman home was now recognized as one of the happiest as well as one of the finest in the city of Oakland. Mr. Huffman was well known throughout the city as a man of sterling integrity and large business acumen, and prosperity had smiled upon him from the first day that he turned his feet to the way of Christianity. The past had been forgotten, but not until Mr. Huffman had made restitution, so far as he could, for everything he had ever taken from a fellow man. He had gone to the man whose home he and Harold Wilson had entered, and confessed his part, and paid back, with compound interest, the money he had taken.

Why, then, should he be anxious?—Ah, for Harold's sake! He had trusted that God would help him to redeem his old pal in sin, and lead him to be a fellow worker in righteousness. But Harold had come, had fallen even lower; and perhaps the uncorrected and unforgiven past, now coming to light, would serve to defeat the purpose he had in mind.

Reaching San Francisco, Mr. Huffman hastened to the police station, and asked to interview the prisoner; his name gave him easy access.

What a picture met his gaze as he looked upon his companion of former years! Brutality seemed stamped upon every feature. But the adage, "So long as there's life, there's hope," buoyed him up; and with loving interest, he sought to have Harold understand that he still trusted him and would stand by him in this hour of need.

Inquiry revealed the fact that Harold had not actually had a part in the murder, yet the circumstances were such as to cause the hand of the law to be laid heavily upon him. Howard Huffman now endeavored to lighten the penalty.

The story of the steps he took to secure his end need not be given. Suffice it to say here that Harold Wilson received freedom only on condition that he leave the country for five years, and with the admonition that when he should return, it must be with a recommendation of good behavior from his employers.

These conditions made him almost a man without a country, and they seemed hard indeed to meet; but through Howard Huffman's encouragement, he determined to try.

He obtained a position as common sailor on the "Pacific Clipper" which sailed from San Francisco to Yokohama one week later; but little did he suspect that the captain of that vessel was his old friend, Captain Mann, of the trip of many years before.

Harold left the Huffman home in Oakland for San Francisco, where his ship lay at the wharf, ready to leave on the morrow. As he passed into the waiting room at the Oakland mole, he observed a "Free Literature" distributor, in one receptacle of which was a Bible; and seeing it, he was struck with its likeness to the one his mother had given him.

Taking the Good Book from its place, he opened it, and, lo, found it to be *marked!* And it was not only marked, but marked much as the other had been marked!

Forgetting all else,—forgetting that he was waiting for the ferry boat, that he was a man banished because of crime, and that he was an almost helpless wreck of humanity,—he sank into a seat, and for a long hour he searched back and forth through that Bible. Yes, many of the same texts were marked; and opposite the message of Exodus 20:8-11 were these words written in the margin: "God's blessing upon the Sabbath is His presence in the Sabbath. He who keeps Sabbath has God's presence in the heart; and all who have His presence will delight to keep Sabbath. Isaiah 58:13." How much this sounded like his mother! And there was Psalm 107:23-31 marked with red ink, the only text marked in red by his dear mother.

He was deeply stirred. A tear stole down his cheek. A vision of a new life floated before him. And in it all, his mother spoke again, and the Christ she loved made His appeal to a lost soul.

"This Bible! O mother, may I take it with me? How can I go without it? It was marked for me. Surely it must have been. Mother, did *you* mark *this* Bible, too?" He spoke thus to himself aloud.

"Friend," a voice spoke from behind, "take the Book. It *was* marked for you. Take it, and God bless you with a knowledge of its truth, and give you a Christian life."

Startled and embarrassed, Harold turned himself, but only to be comforted. The kind face of a father and friend beamed upon him.

He quickly arose, and addressing the stranger, said:

"Do you mean it, sir? May I have this Bible? But, sir, I have no money with which to pay for it."

"That matters nothing, my friend. I represent a people who love God's word, and who are seeking to carry its truth to the whole world. They will be happy to know that this Book is keeping company with one in need. But what did you mean by referring to another marked Bible? Pardon my overhearing."

He was in the company of a true friend; and with brokenness of heart, he told the whole sad story of his battle against his mother, the Bible, and God, and particularly how he had thrown into the sea the sacred gift of his mother's sacrifice and love.

Only a brief interview was possible; but during the few minutes that the two men spent together, Harold Wilson caught a glimpse of the plan of salvation. He saw God's law in its completeness. He saw sin as its transgression. He saw Christ as the One who redeems from the curse.

A word of prayer was offered for Harold by that friend and father—a prayer which he would never forget. Especially did he take to heart this sentence: "Give him rest, Lord, from all evil habits." Of course, it seemed a strange idea, but only to be the longer remembered.

"On what vessel do you sail, young man?" asked the old gentleman as they were parting.

"The 'Pacific Clipper,' sir."

"Ah, that is interesting! She sails tomorrow. Some friends of mine have engaged passage on her, and you must be sure to meet them."

With the treasured Bible in his grip, Harold was soon aboard the ferry. Great experiences were in store for him.

CHAPTER IV

On the Upward Way

"ALMOST eight years," thought Harold, "eight years, almost to a day, since I left here on the 'Alaska Transport' for Melbourne!" The "Pacific Clipper" had just slipped her cables, and was gliding out into San Francisco Bay and under the Golden Gate Bridge, on her long journey to Japan.

"How well I remember that May morning of eight years ago, when, a drunkard, a criminal, a hardened and unhappy wretch, I went to sea to escape justice, and to rid myself of mother's pleadings!

"How well I remember the something that made me want to go back to home and mother, that something which I fought off until I cared for nothing but drink, profanity, and evil company!

"And how vividly I recall the day of the fire, when I found Captain Mann praying, asking God to deliver us from explosion and death!

"Yes, and I remember all too well that hateful minute when I threw my Bible overboard. O God, help me! Why did I do it? I wish I could forget it.

"Now I am starting on another trip, not because I wish, but because I must. I am compelled to leave America, to remain away until I have demonstrated that I am a man worth trusting. But I have no mother; and no friends, I suppose.

"No friends? Yes, I have one—I have that Bible. It seems like mother to me. I just feel, somehow, that it is going to help me to be a better man.

"That old man at the pier was a good man. He seemed to understand me. When he prayed, something gripped my heart; and when he told me I could take the Bible with me, I made up my mind really to try to be decent. I really thought I could be.

"But he certainly did say some queer things. I never heard anything like them before. Yes, yes, I did. I remember that mother used to tell me that we ought to keep the Ten Commandments, all of them. And she said she didn't understand why it was that Christian people kept Sunday when the commandments say we should observe the seventh day. But that old gentleman keeps the day mother thought people ought to keep.

"The queer thing about this whole business is the Bible he gave me. In the first place, it looks like the one I threw away; and besides, it is marked almost the same—the same texts, the same kind of ink, explanations in the margin, and a message written on the flyleaf. But -

"What's that!" He now spoke aloud.

From the thoughts of his important duties (he had been assigned a position on the main deck, forward), and from the reflections regarding his past life, he had suddenly been aroused by a voice, which seemed like a ghost of times long since gone.

He glanced back, but, seeing no one, concluded he must have been mistaken.

But again he heard it! And this time, he looked toward the bridge. There stood Captain Mann!

Yes, it was the same old captain, the hero of the "Alaska Transport," who was now in command of this great transpacific passenger liner.

Harold Wilson was almost overcome with emotion. His heart palpitated with joy. Deep in his heart there was a something which seemed to tell him that during this journey across the sea, he was to learn the secret of a better life, and that the man of prayer on the bridge had been given to aid him.

It was several days before the opportunity came to the young man to meet and greet the man he so much revered. Duty finally brought them into contact, and Harold fairly rushed to grasp the captain's hand.

"Captain Mann! Thank God for the chance to sail with you again!"

The captain's big, wholehearted hand gladly grasped Harold's, reciprocating fully the spirit of good will evinced; but his face wore a puzzled look.

"My young man, why do you thank God? When I knew you, you had no regard for God."

"Yes, captain; but I have fought long enough what I know is right. I want to find God, and know Him just as you did that day the fire broke out on the 'Alaska Transport.' I want to know and serve Him just as my mother did. Do you remember the talk you gave us about the Bible and its promises?"

"Yes, but I have no memory it did you any good."

"That is true, captain; for that very day, I went and hatefully threw into the sea the Bible my dear mother gave me. And she had marked it for me, too. Do you know, she had marked in it that very verse that you said saved us from the fire!

"But, Captain Mann, I have another Bible, and one that is marked. That verse in the Psalms is marked, the Ten Commandments are marked, yes, and a great number of other texts!"

"Where did you find such a Bible, my boy?" the captain kindly inquired.

Then Harold told the sad story of his mother's death, his abandonment to sin, his arrest, his sentence, and the discovery of the Bible, and the meeting of the old gentleman at the Oakland pier.

"Oh, yes," said the captain, "I know of that gentleman. He belongs to a very peculiar people, who keep Saturday instead of Sunday; and he has placed in the reading room of this vessel a large number of papers and leaflets for the benefit of our passengers and crew."

"Well, captain, he found me reading the Bible at the pier; and when he saw that I was longing for it, he let me bring it with me. I tell you, he was the best man I ever met. He understood me. And when I told him how far down I had gone, he had a little tear for me, and prayed that I might find deliverance from all my wrong habits, and have rest in Christ. What he said to me seemed to open up the whole plan of right living, and I made up my mind to try to be a better man. And I want you to help me, captain."

"I certainly will do my best to aid you to become a Christian; but I fear I shall not be able to help you to believe as that old gentleman believes, for I think he is wrong about the keeping of Saturday. There are a number of his people aboard the vessel, though—missionaries to the Philippines; and they will help you. But look out, my boy, and don't go wild."

CHAPTER V

A Real Missionary

THE "Pacific Clipper" had been plowing her way through the waters for a week, when one day a pleasant-looking man came up to Harold, and without introduction, very kindly asked him if he was a Christian. This was the first time in all his life that such a question had been brought home to him. But though greatly astonished, Harold was pleased to be thus directly questioned by the stranger.

"No, sir," he replied, "I am not; but I am just now thinking I ought to be. And what is your name, sir?"

"My name is Anderson."

"Are you one of the missionaries going to the Philippines, sir?"

"Yes; and why do you ask?"

"Well, Captain Mann has told me that there were missionaries aboard, and I have been wanting to see one of them and ask some questions. You see, I have with me a Bible given me by an old gentleman at the Oakland pier. This Bible is marked. It is marked almost the same as one my Christian mother gave me, but which I threw into the sea because I hated Christianity. The marking therefore takes me back to my old home, to things my mother said, and I want someone to help me know how to begin a true Christian life."

"Is your name Wilson, my young friend?" the gentleman inquired. "Harold Wilson?"

"Yes, sir; but how did you learn my name?"

"It is a rather strange story, but I will tell you. A few days before I left Oakland, I saw in a San Francisco paper the report of a certain trial, that of a young man by the name of Wilson, who had been sentenced, because of some wrongdoing, to a five-year absence from the country. The reporter made note of various extenuating circumstances, of a good mother's dying prayer, and of the hope of strong, good friends, that the young man would turn and become an honor to his parents, both of whom had devotedly given him to God. It was stated that the young man would have a position aboard the 'Pacific Clipper,' the vessel on which I was to make my trip to the Orient; and I determined to try to meet him and help him as I could."

Harold carefully eyed this new friend; for had not Captain Mann cautioned him against being led off into wild notions? Yet Mr. Anderson had a good face, a sincere expression, and apparently unselfish interest. And, really, it seemed to Harold that it was more than a mere happening that he had been led to meet him.

"You did not know my mother, did you? She was a great believer in doing just what the Bible says, and was always urging me to follow it. She lived in San Francisco."

"Was her first name Helen?" Mr. Anderson inquired.

"Yes, yes! Did you know her?"

"My boy, your mother was a member of my church.

As her pastor, I have more than once heard her tell of her wandering child, and of her constant prayer that he would one day become acquainted with the Lord Jesus. She told of the Bible she had purchased, of the message she had written, of the texts she had marked, of the explanation she had placed in the margins. She believed it would one day touch his heart. But for long years, she heard nothing from him, and finally she gave him up as lost at sea. When stricken down with illness, and on her deathbed, she called the old brother whom you met at the Oakland pier, and asked him to place in the distributor another Bible, marked as she had marked that one years before. And are you her son, Harold?"

"Indeed I am, sir; and now I believe you have been sent to show me the way to Christ. Oh, Mr. Anderson, if there is a remedy for my follies, I want it, and I want it now! I'm a thief, a drunkard, a gambler, a wretch without a country, a sinner without a God. Can you help me?"

The finding of Harold Wilson seemed so wonderfully beautiful to Mr. Anderson, so providential, so timely, that his faith laid hold upon the promise of God; and in a wise, tactful, soul-winning way, he led him to the Master's feet. The surrender was complete, founded on an intelligent grasp of revealed truth; and the young man was happy in God.

When the story of Harold's life and conversion came to be known, he was pointed out by both passengers and crew as "the man with the marked Bible."

Captain Mann, while a devoted Christian, was nevertheless quite limited in his knowledge of the Scriptures, and therefore a bit narrow. Thus it was that he now became much concerned lest Harold should be deluded by the "false teachings" of Mr. Anderson, and especially when he learned of the frequent appointments Harold was making with him; and he sought to counteract the pastor's influence.

"What does this mean?" thought Harold to himself, as he meditated upon Captain Mann's opposition. "Here are two good men, both of whom seem honest, yet each one is certain that the other is wrong. I am sure Captain Mann had his prayers answered and saved my life, and I am sure Mr. Anderson has had his prayers answered in leading me to be a Christian. What shall I do? I certainly cannot follow both, for they seem to be going in opposite directions.

"But after all, I'll do what my mother used to urge me to do. I'll just have to take the Bible for myself."

But if the captain lacked in knowledge, he did not lack in an enthusiastic interest to see that Harold did not become "entangled with false ideas about the Sabbath." It came to pass, however, that his earnest efforts to save the young man from delusion only hastened forward the work of truth which God desired to have wrought.

"Young man" (this was the captain's favorite form of address), "let me counsel you again to be careful about this matter of the day you keep."

"But, Captain Mann, why do you speak this way? No one has said anything to me about keeping Saturday."

"Well, you will find that Mr. Anderson will soon be telling you that if you are to live a Christian life, you must keep the day that his church keeps. He will tell you that Sunday isn't mentioned in the Bible, and—"

"Really, captain, is Sunday not spoken of in the Bible? I shall be glad to have you show me the matter as it is before Mr. Anderson gets to it, if you think best."

"All right; come in this evening, and I will show you that Mr. Anderson's church is wrong."

CHAPTER VI

An Embarrassed Captain

"THAT makes me think," said Harold as the captain passed on. "I remember that he told me they had put aboard a supply of reading matter. I wonder if there is anything about Sunday. I will ask Mr. Anderson about it." He found him aft.

"Mr. Anderson, do you suppose your people have placed aboard this vessel, with other literature, anything about Sunday?"

"Why, yes, Harold, I presume they have. But what causes you to be interested about Sunday? You keep Sunday, do you not?"

"Oh, yes; but you see, Captain Mann is afraid that I will not keep on in that way, and tonight he is going to show me that the Bible says Sunday is the right day. He said you would soon be telling me that Sunday is not mentioned in the Bible, and he wants to prove that it is. Of course, I think I should find out all I can for myself before I meet him this evening. What should I look for?"

"Well, there are several little leaflets you may well read, such as 'Which Day Do You Keep, and Why?'

and 'Sunday in the New Testament.' I think you will find them in that supply. If you do not, come to me, and I will try to assist you."

While Harold was searching for these leaflets, Captain Mann had found a bit of leisure time for putting into shape the thoughts he would present to Harold. He thought he knew in general what would aid the young man, so he set about to find the specific texts he would use.

It had been several years since the question of the Sabbath had agitated him; and never, in fact, had he attempted to locate the passages in which the word "Sunday" occurred. He felt quite certain, though, that they were in the Gospels, and in the story of the resurrection. But after much careful searching, he did not find what he was after.

"I have probably forgotten the connections," he said to himself, as he turned to his concordance.

But even Cruden, for some reason, had overlooked the Sunday passages. To be sure, Cruden did not profess to give every word in the Bible.

"Sunday, S-u-n-d-a-y—where did I see it?" he said. "The young man will think it very strange in me to call him in here to do something I cannot do."

Then a happy thought occurred to him. "There is Mr. Mitchell, an old orthodox minister. I will ask him, and also get other helpful information."

Mr. Mitchell welcomed the captain to his stateroom, pleased to be honored by a call from the now famous captain.

"Pardon me, Mr. Mitchell," the captain said, "but I am here to ask a personal favor. As you may know, we have on board, as a member of my crew, a young man who has just experienced a remarkable conversion. You may have heard him mentioned as 'the man with the marked Bible.' He has an interesting history. We also have aboard, as a passenger, a certain Mr. Anderson, of the seventh-day people, who seems to have this young man under his influence, and who, I am sure, will sooner or later seek to trouble him over the Sabbath matter. So I am taking an interest in the case. I have asked the young man to call on me this evening, and I have promised to show him that Sunday is the true day of worship. Now, what I wish you to do is to put me in touch with all the texts in which Sunday is mentioned."

Was it a smile, a frown, or a look of disappointment and chagrin that stole over Mr. Mitchell's face as he heard the captain's request? Whatever it was, it did not express pleasure.

"Captain," said he, "there are no such texts. You will have to acknowledge that the word 'Sunday' is not between the two lids of the Book of God."

"But, Mr. Mitchell, I could almost take an oath that I have seen it and read it."

"Not in the Bible, captain. You will find mention, a few times, of the first day of the week, but not of Sunday; and even the first day of the week is not spoken of as being sacred. You have undertaken a difficult task in attempting to show reasons for Sundaykeeping from the Scriptures."

Though he had lived sixty years, Captain Mann had never heard even a hint of this which Mr. Mitchell had now so boldly asserted. He was shocked, if not almost stunned. It could not be true, he reasoned. Was he himself the deluded one? He hesitated.

Mr. Mitchell was a man of brilliant intellect. For more than thirty years he had stood before the public, and he was known in both Occident and Orient as a fearless defender of the church and its work. With infidel, with atheist, with foe in and out of the church, he had never feared to battle, and he had not failed to win laurels. However, he had always and consistently refused to enter into argument with the Sabbatarians, for he knew the impossibility of making good his case. It was only logical, therefore, that he addressed the captain as he did, and bluntly stated the truth he knew.

Seeing that the captain had been greatly perturbed by his plain, matter-of-fact statement, he proceeded to explain why, without a "Thus saith the Lord," he still observed the first day of the week.

"Captain," he continued, "any reliable student of church history will tell you that there is only one foundation for our practice of Sunday worship, and that is the custom of the early church. Both Christ and His apostles, and those immediately associated with them, believed in and practiced the observance of the seventh day of the week, the Sabbath of the fourth commandment; and not for several hundred years after Christ was there any such thing known as a sacred regard for Sunday. The change was brought about gradually, through the influence of churchmen; but we must not suppose that they had divine sanction for it. It was simply the outgrowth of a change in the spirit of the times.

"Over and over again I have had to tell my friends in private what I have said to you. And I have said to them what I must now say to you also—that though the change came about in a way with which we might not really agree, yet it came, and the only reasonable course for us to take is to endorse it and go ahead with God's great church to evangelize the world. It is too late now to attempt a reformation.

"And now a bit of advice: Give the matter a wide

berth. The agitation of the question only creates many embarrassing situations, and gives the few who still believe in the absolute requirements of the moral law an opportunity to advance their arguments, which are practically unanswerable. I think you will readily see my point. Deftly turn the young man aside with the thought that God is love, that He has led His church throughout the ages and still leads it, and that while we may not be able to explain all, we may safely go ahead with the great work of preaching Christ, and wait another time to have some of our queries removed. This usually satisfies, and undoubtedly will in this case."

"Thank you, doctor," was the captain's response as he politely withdrew and returned to his stateroom.

Meanwhile Harold Wilson had been finding some very interesting material regarding the origin of Sunday observance, though it did not mean as much to him at that time as it did later. His spiritual eyes were just beginning to open, and he saw but little. However, he was blessed by what he did see, and had become anxious to meet the captain and hear what he would say.

Mr. Anderson smiled, yet seriously, at what the captain had thought to do. Thousands of equally honest and devout men had attempted the same thing before, but only to find and obey the truth, or else plunge deeply into willing ignorance and dishonest opposition. He was much interested to hear what Captain Mann would say.

Ill at ease, indeed, was the captain; for not only had he been rudely awakened to the fact that he had long believed what was not true, but he had also been counseled by an ambassador of Christ to practice what seemed to him a kind of dishonesty. He had always prized his own sincerity, and he would continue to do so. This was his decision: He would meet Harold Wilson, and acknowledge that there was no mention of Sunday in the Bible. Further than this he could not see; for he still believed, notwithstanding the minister, that Sunday was sacred.

Harold came, with his Bible in his hand, with leaflets in his pockets, with the beginnings of truth in his soul. He seated himself with an air of expectancy.

"Young man,"—the captain came at once to the point, —"I want to tell you, right at the first, that I have been mistaken in regard to Sunday's being mentioned in the Bible. It isn't there. The first day of the week is spoken of a great many times, and it was this I had in mind. So I acknowledge my error. But my mistake does not alter the fact that the Lord Jesus changed the day, and that His apostles afterward looked upon the first day of the week, the day of the resurrection, as the Lord's day, and held their meetings on that day."

"How many times, captain, do you think the first day is mentioned?"

"Oh, a great many times, I should naturally suppose! Of course, I cannot give the exact number."

Harold pulled from his pocket a small leaflet, and proceeded to read from it.

"This shows that it is mentioned only eight times, and that in not one case is it spoken of as sacred. Maybe this isn't true; but it gives the references, and asks us to look them up. Here they are: Matthew 28:1; Mark 16:2, 9; Luke 24:1; John 20:1, 19; Acts 20:7; and 1 Corinthians 16:2. Suppose we read them, captain."

One by one the eight passages were found and read.

"Now, captain, you are acquainted with the Bible, and I am not. You must therefore let me ask a few questions, in order that I may find out what I want to know. So will you please tell me which of these references show that the first day of the week took the place of the seventh as the Sabbath day?"

Captain Mann pointed to the meeting of the apostles on the resurrection day, and said: "It seems clear that they were holding some kind of service in honor of His resurrection; for it says (Luke 24:36) that Jesus stood in the midst of them, and said, 'Peace be unto you.' At this time, He breathed upon them the Holy Ghost, and sent them forth to preach that He was risen. Do you not think this a reasonable explanation?"

"That sounds all right, captain; but here is something you overlooked." Again Harold referred to the leaflet. "I see here that when the disciples met that night, they were having their supper (Mark 16:14); and when Jesus came, they gave Him some broiled fish and some honeycomb (Luke 24:42). They had the doors barred for fear of the Jews. John 20:19. They did not believe He was risen; for when He appeared to them, they were terrified, thinking they saw a spirit. Luke 24:37. And then Christ reproved them because they believed not (Mark 16:14), and only said, 'Peace be unto you,' to calm their fears. Besides all this, Thomas didn't believe in the resurrection until a number of days later. John 20:24-27.

"Captain, they couldn't have been celebrating the resurrection when they didn't believe in it, could they?"

"Young man, where did you get all this? I never heard these things before. But I must say you seem to be right. I have to be honest.

"There is another text, though," he continued, "which clearly teaches that the believers in the apostles' time observed the first day of the week. Look at Acts 20 again. Here it plainly states that they met on the first day of the week to break bread."

Again the young convert turned to the leaflet in his

hand, and then he said: "Captain, that meeting must have been on Saturday night, for it was on the dark part of the first day of the week, and the dark part of the day comes first. Genesis 1:5, 8, etc. Paul preached until midnight because he was going to Assos the next morning. Acts 20:7. Then he ate his supper (verse 11), talked on until daylight, and then, during the light part of Sunday, walked nineteen miles across the isthmus to Assos. He surely didn't keep the day as a sacred day. It rather looks as though it was a special meeting, called at an irregular time in order to accommodate Paul, and the breaking of bread was to satisfy hunger rather than to commemorate the Lord's death."

At this point, the gong sounded for change of watch, and Harold hastened away to duty.

Captain Mann seemed almost dazed. The thought of having been wrong in his ideas for so many years and that a minister of the gospel had advised him to close his eyes to admitted errors, was almost too much for him.

"Can it be," he said aloud to himself, "that I am wrong also in other things? If I could be so entirely out of line concerning those simple texts regarding the resurrection, then in other matters not so simple I may be still farther away from the right,

"Very shortly, if God permits it, I shall have another interview with Mr. Mitchell. I intend to get at the bottom of this thing."

CHAPTER VII

An Embarrassed Minister

I T WAS no idle resolution which Captain Mann formed when he determined to go again to Mr. Mitchell in order to get to the bottom of some of the matters that were agitating his mind; and after leaving Honolulu, he found his opportunity.

The "Pacific Clipper" was one of the largest and finest passenger vessels that plied the waters of the Pacific, and the responsibilities of its captain were tremendous in both their number and their weight. There was not an hour of the day or of the night when he was out from under the burden of his vessel's care. Nevertheless, Captain Mann was able to interest himself in the needs of his passengers and crew, and many a soul was blessed by his kindly presence and unselfish helpfulness.

Never before, however, had he been so stirred by any question, personal or otherwise, as by this which had arisen over the experience of Harold Wilson. At every hour of the day it pressed in upon his mind, and he sought every opportunity to investigate and pray about it. In fact, it had brought a crisis into his life.

For many years, he had set apart as sacred a small portion of each day for Bible reading and prayer. The next afternoon, the hour for personal devotion having come, as he was about to enter his stateroom he met Mr. Mitchell. This was the time, he reasoned, to carry out his purpose; and the two were soon seated and engaged in conversation.

"Mr. Mitchell," said the captain, "do you believe in the binding moral obligations of the Ten Commandments?"

"Yes, captain, I most certainly do."

"Do you endorse the idea that the Bible as a whole is the authoritative word of God, given by inspiration as our guide?"

"Most assuredly. There is no other safe position to take. No man who allows himself to discount any portion of the good old Book can meet the attacks of the atheist or the infidel."

"Pardon me, doctor; but may I ask then, pointedly, how you harmonize this view with your statement that we had better ignore the question of the Sabbath and go on quietly in the keeping of Sunday, though admitting there is no Bible foundation for doing so? It seems to me you play fast and loose."

"Well, captain, when I say that I believe in the binding moral obligations of the Ten Commandments, I must except the fourth, for this is not moral in the same sense as are the other nine. The claims of the Sabbath commandment are satisfied just as fully by the setting apart of the first day of the week as of the seventh. The time feature of the fourth commandment is not necessarily moral."

"Mitchell," said the captain very earnestly, "do you mean to tell me that concrete terms, such as, 'The seventh day is the Sabbath of the Lord thy God: in it thou shalt not do any work,' are not necessarily moral? Has God no power to incorporate moral principle in the specific and limiting word 'seventh'?

"Let me illustrate my point: I have under me a large force of men manning this vessel. For the safety of all aboard, I am required to hold frequent fire drills, and I issue orders to the engineer to blow the fire whistle at twelve o'clock sharp Tuesday noon. Having done this, I arrange all my plans accordingly, making everything fit into a particular minute. Supremely important is that minute to me, to my crew, to my passengers, and to my company. And that engineer is under solemn contract to carry out my instructions, whether or not my reasons are known or understood. In such case, you are bound to admit that a moral obligation, of which time is almost the entire value, is binding an inferior to obey his superior. And you will not even hint that the engineer or anyone else may reasonably or rightly decide that some other minute will fulfill my purpose.

"The fourth commandment is the commandment of all the ten, it seems to me, most vitally charged with moral principle, because of its specific time element. You see, men may differ over such matters as what constitutes a lie, or what is comprehended in hatred, or what is profanity; but they simply cannot argue over the meaning of such a term as 'seventh.'

"Why, Mitchell, I was taught this by my mother; and all my life I have found in the Sabbath commandment my strong fortress of absolute integrity. It has been righteousness expressed in figures; and figures are not very often found lying.

"Of course, I have always believed that when Jesus came, He changed the day of rest from the seventh day of the week to the first. This did not trouble me, for I believed that He who set apart the seventh day in olden time as a day of worship and rest, had a right to sanctify and bless the first day of the week in later time, just as I would have a right to change an appointment from noon on Tuesday to noon on Wednesday.

"But you are the first one to tell me that no moral value attaches to the matter of time. You are the first minister to put forth the idea that the fourth commandment is an exception, and that in a sense it is unmoral. The whole Bible is inspired, yet you permit your human *reasoning* to nullify a portion of the only words directly spoken by God Himself to the human ear.

"Again I beg your pardon, but let me suggest this query: If, as you say, the Bible is the authoritative word of God; if the Ten Commandments are unchangeably binding in their moral claims; if neither Jesus Christ nor His apostles made a change in the day of the Sabbath; if the observance of Sunday rests only on early custom—if all these things be true, then are you and I not under solemn covenant obligation to keep the fourth commandment?

"Mitchell, I did not accept your counsel of yesterday; and when I met the young man last evening, I was constrained to acknowledge myself mistaken. No man who recognizes that his soul is at stake in this great life game will ever knowingly do evil that good may come.

"I am still hoping to get hold of evidence that at the cross a new era was introduced, and that since that time the followers of Christ, under the new covenant, are to honor 'the Lord's day,' the day of the resurrection. But mark this: If I find that in this, too, I have been mistaken, and that the Bible is silent concerning a change of the time of the Sabbath, I shall gladly and with all my heart take up my cross anew and keep the Sabbath."

Apparently Mr. Mitchell was not disposed to take the captain's earnest and logical remarks very seriously, and they were not allowed to banish his accustomed smile. When the captain had finished, the minister only said: "Well, you are surely my superior in argument, and I must attempt no reply. You may rest assured, though, that if you stand by your reasoning, you will be obliged to keep the Jewish Sabbath."

At this point Mr. Mitchell found it necessary to be excused and, with a cheerful "So long," he made his exit. The truth of the matter was, he felt himself distinctly embarrassed, and wished to avoid further probing at the captain's hands.

As the minister withdrew, Harold Wilson made a brief call to inform the captain that since they had talked the day before, he had found "a lot of new things."

"Have you been talking to Mr. Anderson, young man?" the captain inquired.

"No; but I have been reading my Bible and talking to people I have met. And, captain, this Sabbath question is a mighty interesting subject. Everyone wants to know about it. Did you know that there are three other preachers aboard?"

The captain well knew this, but his experience with Mr. Mitchell had somewhat discouraged him.

"One of those preachers, Dr. Spaulding, is a great talker, captain. When he heard me talking to some of the men, he acted as though he had some bad blood. Why, he almost jumped at me and said that anyone who kept the old Jewish Sabbath was 'almost a Christ killer,' if you know what that means.

"Well, I didn't know at first what to say, so I let him talk on until I got my breath.

"By and by I asked him what he meant by the 'Jewish

Sabbath.' I said, 'Do you mean the Sabbath of the fourth commandment?'

" 'Yes, sir,' he said, 'that's exactly what I mean. The Ten Commandments were given to the Jews; and when Christ came and died, they were all nailed to the cross. The Sabbath lived and died with that Christless nation.'

"Just then Mr. Anderson came along, and I couldn't help asking him what he thought. You see, I had never heard about a Jewish Sabbath, or in fact, any other particular kind of Sabbath, so I wanted to have the preachers make it clear.

"The first thing Anderson did was to ask Dr. Spaulding why he called it 'Jewish.'

" 'Because, with all the other commandments of the old law, it was given to the Jews,' he replied. 'And that whole code was abolished at the cross.' "

"That is what I have always understood," said the captain, interrupting Harold's narration.

"But you won't believe it longer, I think," said Harold, "after you've heard the story.

"Anderson asked, 'Do you believe, then, that today there is no law against stealing and murdering, and that there is no longer any obligation for children to honor father and mother?'

"Dr. Spaulding then said something that did not amount to much, for he seemed unable to explain; and Anderson inquired: 'What do you preach to people when you wish them to accept Christ? Do you not tell them they are sinners? You certainly do; but the moment you say this, you are denying your theory, for men are sinners only when they have transgressed the law. Paul says, you know, that "sin is not imputed when there is no law." '

"A crowd began to gather while Anderson was speaking, and Dr. Spaulding asked to be excused; but we all insisted he ought to help finish the conversation he had begun, so he stayed.

" 'Now, brother,' Anderson said, 'this has always been true. The only reason why Adam was a sinner was that he transgressed law. All through the history of time, there has been sin; and all through the history of time, therefore, there has been law—God's moral law. Thus all through the history of time, likewise, there has been a Saviour to redeem man from the law's condemnation. Law, sin, Saviour—these are the three great outstanding facts in the Bible story.'

"I gave him my Bible to read his proof from, and he surely gave plenty. He read a text for every statement he made. 1 John 3:4 showed sin to be transgression; Romans 5:13, that there cannot be sin without law; and Romans 5:12, that Adam sinned; and Revelation 13:8, that Christ has been a Saviour from the very first."

The captain picked up his own Bible, and read Revelation 13:8; for it came to him as a text scarcely known before.

"That does say, young man, that Christ was slain from the foundation of the world, doesn't it? But I do not exactly understand it."

"Well, Anderson explained it by saying that all the time before Christ came, people had the gospel, and were saved by faith in a Redeemer to come. He read Galatians 3:8 and John 8:56 to show that Abraham knew Christ, and Hebrews 11:26 to show that Moses did. A man couldn't help but see it.

"Then he showed that Christ was the One who gave the Sabbath in the beginning, that it was Christ who spoke the Ten Commandments, and that it was Christ who went with the Israelites through all their journeys.

Of course, Dr. Spaulding didn't enjoy it all; but he had to acknowledge that what was said was true, for it was all there in the Bible.

"I couldn't help laughing when, at the last, Anderson asked: 'Spaulding, if Christ made the worlds (and you admit that He did), and if it was He who made the Sabbath and gave it to man (and you admit that, too), and if He spoke the law on Sinai, and thus gave the Sabbath again, must it not be that the Sabbath known back there was the Sabbath of Christ, and therefore the Christian Sabbath?' Spaulding blushed, and moved in an odd, nervous way, and then we all laughed. But he said 'Yes' just the same. He couldn't help it.

"Before we left, Anderson said this: 'Friends, I am sure you can all see that the term "Jewish Sabbath" is an expression which Christians should not use any more than they should say "the Jewish law of God." Both the law and the Sabbath, which is a part of it, were given at the very beginning, 2,500 years before the Jewish nation existed. The Sabbath was given to the whole human race; or, as Jesus said, it "was made for man." Mark 2:27.'

"Dr. Spaulding was excited when we broke up, and he said to us: 'This has been a kind of one-sided discussion today; but if any of you want to study this further, come here tomorrow at two o'clock, and I will show you a few things. You will then see that this seventh-day business is a pretty small affair.'"

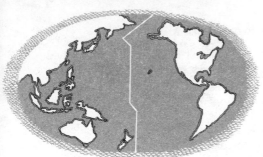

CHAPTER VIII

Theological Disagreement and Confusion

HUMAN nature enjoys a fray; and as the word was passed around among the passengers that Dr. Spaulding intended to take the theological warpath, a buzz of excitement was at once created, and here and there little groups could be seen discussing what might happen the next day.

Captain Mann wore a smiling face and maintained a strictly neutral air, but inwardly he was sharing the spirit of intensity which seemed to have taken possession of many of the passengers.

Dr. Spaulding, immediately after his conversation with Mr. Anderson, in which he had felt his position rudely shaken, sought out his fellow ministers and invited them to his room for a consultation.

The veil of secrecy must of necessity be thrown around much that took place as the three clerical brethren met and considered the situation. Suffice it here to say that when Mr. Mitchell learned, after his arrival, the purpose of the meeting, he devoutly wished himself elsewhere. He distinctly saw that his brother minister had made a mistake, and that unless much care and wisdom were exercised, great embarrassment was sure to follow.

That which most distressed them all in their planning was the fact that they seemed utterly unable to agree among themselves. Dr. Spaulding believed that the Sabbath had been abolished at the cross; Mr. Mitchell held that it had been changed by the early church; while Mr. Gregory was bound to teach that the seventh day of the fourth commandment should be observed, but that Sunday was the true seventh day.

Seeing the hopelessness of reconciling these divergent and conflicting views, Mr. Mitchell finally ventured to repeat the advice he had given Captain Mann; namely, that the wise course to take would be to ignore the question and emphasize such points as God's love and world evangelization, and thus cause the ordinary inquirer to forget and pass on.

"But, Mitchell, I cannot do that," interposed Dr. Spaulding. "I have put myself on record and have openly announced that at two o'clock I will meet all who are interested. I have to do something."

"Yet you will find, brother, that if you attempt to show that the moral law has been abolished, you have brought the whole question into a tremendous tangle. Why, you can see that as soon as you claim the abolition of the whole law, just to get rid of the Sabbath, you have really taken from us the only standard of righteous living ever given to the world." Thus spoke Mr. Gregory.

"Oh, no, brother! for we now have the new law, and are under its jurisdiction," said Dr. Spaulding.

"Well, I have heard that argument over and over," replied Mr. Gregory, "but always to be convinced more fully of its weakness, if not of its absurdity. Did not Jesus Christ clearly teach, all through the Sermon on the Mount, the inviolability of the law? Read Matthew 5: 17, 18, and onward, and see. And did not Paul, by inspiration, make the decided statement that faith establishes the law? See Romans 3:31. Then listen to James, who actually quotes the sixth and the seventh commandments, thus showing what law he means, and, in close connection, directly calls it 'the royal law,' 'the law of liberty,' the law by which men are finally to be judged. James 2:8-12. Brother, the 'new law' of which you speak is only the Decalogue made new by the life and power of Jesus Christ. And that old law made new includes the Sabbath, and no one can escape it. Cannot you see that?"

"But, my dear friend," Dr. Spaulding very earnestly responded, "if you take that position, you will certainly have to surrender our custom of Sunday worship; for there is absolutely no doubt that Saturday is the seventh day of the week and therefore the day to be kept according to the commandment. The only way to avoid the seventh day is to be freed from the commandment itself.

"You are hitting pretty hard, my brother," said Mr. Gregory, with some show of warmth, "and I am not sure that you are not doing me a bit of injustice. You forget, I think, that more than once the calendar has been changed, and that days have been added or dropped in order to make proper adjustments."

"Very true, good friend; but you are surely not so ignorant (pardon my plainness) as to suppose that changes of calendar affected the order of the days of the week. The weekly cycle has never been altered. The Gregorian calendar of A.D. 1582 dropped out ten days; and Thursday, October 4, was followed immediately by Friday, October 15. Russia still followed the old style of reckoning until 1918; but her days of the week were the same as ours.

"Our week, with its seventh day, has come to us without change from time immemorial. I was reading yesterday that of 160 ancient and modern languages and dialects, 108 actually know the seventh day by the name 'Sabbath' or its equivalent; and the writer stated that all of them 'bear testimony to the identity and order of the days of the ancient and modern week.' He also added that the testimony adduced 'is equally positive that the order of the days of the week is the same now as from the beginning of nations.' To my mind, this is incontrovertible evidence. A Sunday Sabbath is impossible."

"You will surely agree with me now that my suggestion made at the beginning of our interview has in it at least a measure of good judgment," interrupted Mr. Mitchell. "I repeat that the situation is one which is embarrassing; and I advise that Dr. Spaulding make an effort to sidetrack the main question and introduce some minor feature tomorrow. To carry these controverted points before any intelligent audience, and especially before one that has in it a man of Anderson's abilities, is but to invite a theological catastrophe."

With this counsel adopted as a basis for the work of the next day, the brethren separated.

There was no lack in interest or attendance when the hour appointed by Dr. Spaulding came.

It was generally understood that he would attack the Sabbath question "without gloves;" and naturally interest centered on Mr. Anderson, for it seemed inconceivable that he would allow Dr. Spaulding's statements to go unchallenged.

Mr. Anderson, however, sat in a somewhat secluded position, evidently having no purpose to enter into controversy. To him, debate was painful, and he avoided it always if possible.

"My Christian friends,"—thus began Dr. Spaulding, —"I am profoundly convinced that many questions relative to our various beliefs can never be fully and satisfactorily settled. In fact, I believe it is not the plan of God that they should be. No one can know absolutely that he is right. All doctrines are relative. Truth today may be error tomorrow.

"The question of the Sabbath is one of the unsettled points of faith. One denomination holds one position, another holds another. The Mohammedan observes Friday; the Jew and the Adventist, Saturday; the Christian world as a whole, Sunday."

"Pardon me, Dr. Spaulding" (the speaker was a scholarly-looking judge of nearly seventy winters, who sat directly in front of the minister), "but do you really mean to have us believe that you think it matters not whether we keep Friday or Sunday, provided we have the right spirit? Did I not hear you say yesterday that if anyone should keep the seventh day he would become 'almost a Christ killer'? You certainly led us to the conclusion that a great deal of importance attached to the matter of which day we keep and that today you would show that the 'seventh-day business,' as you termed it, 'is a pretty small affair.'"

Dr. Spaulding hesitated, and was evidently confused. His well-planned diversion was failing. With difficulty, however, he attempted to proceed.

"Before the interruption, I was about to say that—"

"But, doctor, I insist on an answer. I have good reason for so doing, as you ought to know. Do you now repudiate the doctrine which you at that time endorsed?"

All present now realized the hopelessness of Dr.

Spaulding's position; and while they shared in the judge's desire for fair play, they inwardly longed for something to happen that would relieve the man of his embarrassment. Providentially something did "happen."

"Dr. Spaulding, allowing the judge's question to be answered a little later, may I interrupt to ask if you can give us some light on the subject of the date line? Captain Mann informs me that we are nearing the date line, and that tonight we must drop a day from our reckoning. Tomorrow, therefore, instead of having a Tuesday, we shall have a Wednesday. What effect, as you understand it, does this change have upon the matter of a definite day of the week as Sabbath?"

The questioner was Mr. Severance, a San Francisco merchant who had often made the transpacific trip and who therefore was fully informed regarding the problem of the date line.

Dr. Spaulding quickly brightened at the mention of the date line, and smilingly consented to give his opinion. In fact, he was making an effort to reach this particular point when interrogated by the judge.

"I am glad, sir, to have you introduce this question; and with the judge's permission to pass his question for the present, I will venture a brief statement.

"I suppose all or nearly all are aware that in crossing the Pacific Ocean east or west, a day must be added or dropped. Going west, we are obliged to skip a day; and going east, to repeat a day. For instance, tonight we shall retire during the hours of Monday, and tomorrow morning we shall wake up to find that we are passing through the hours of Wednesday. We shall have no Tuesday at all.

"Now, suppose I ardently believe in the absolute sacredness of Saturday. I am going to the Philippines. I reach the date line Friday evening and begin to keep my Sabbath. Then I retire with a worshipful spirit, anticipating the joys of the holy time for the morrow. I sleep. I wake. It is morning. But, lo, instead of its being Saturday, my good captain tells me it is Sunday!

"Then I become excited and confused. The thing bewilders me. I thought my theory correct, but find it incorrect. The fourth commandment, I discover, doesn't fit a big, round world. My Sabbath slipped away from me without even so much as a farewell. If I keep any day at all, I have to keep Sunday.

"I think you will all agree with me that, if I am ordinarily intelligent, I will come to the conclusion that God never meant that seventh day for me, at least while crossing the Pacific; for when I tried to keep it, I could not."

"May I ask a question?" said Mr. Severance.

"Certainly," replied the minister.

"I observe Sunday and live in San Francisco. Do you believe I really can keep Sunday in that city?"

"Yes; because in San Francisco, the days come to you regularly, and you need not question the order of their recurrence."

"Would it be possible for me to have my Sunday in Tokyo?"

"Certainly," was Dr. Spaulding's answer, "and for the same reason."

"Now, Dr. Spaulding, you say the day travels. It must, then, have some place at which it begins its journey, and likewise some place at which it ends its journey. What place is that? If you are willing to yield the floor for a time, I should like a few words from our captain."

"Captain Mann! Captain Mann!" came the call from all directions. All eyes were turned to him.

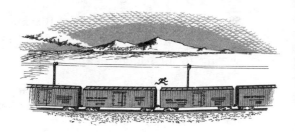

CHAPTER IX

A Ship Captain on the Date Line

"THIS is Dr. Spaulding's hour," the captain began, "and with his permission, I will consent to make a few observations regarding the date line."

Dr. Spaulding smiled faintly, and in a somewhat hesitating manner he seemed to give consent. The entire situation had proved a great disappointment to him; and now he was really obliged to give place, without having made any substantial gain.

As Captain Mann arose, a happy thought seemed to strike him, and he smilingly suggested a round table, or question box, that thus all might have opportunity to bring out any phase of the question not clear to them. The question-box idea prevailed.

"Before the questions are proposed," said the captain, "allow me this brief word: The date line is one of the simple problems of life, so simple, in fact, that I have often explained it without difficulty to children. Instead of its being a matter for confusing minds and causing a loss in the count of the days of the week, it is the one thing that prevents any and all disturbances in our reckoning. It is a great, wonderful world regulator, preserving to all nations of the earth the identity of our days."

"Do you mean to say, captain, that the fact that the world is a globe makes no difference?" asked a woman missionary from Ohio.

"That is the thought, madam. It matters not whether one is at the poles or at the equator, whether traveling by sea or by land, whether going east or going west, the day is an absolutely fixed quantity of time, and may be scientifically and accurately known at any place on the earth's surface."

"Well, I have heard it said, over and over," stated a simple but well-meaning man seated near the captain, "that time is really lost or gained—that going in one direction, you lose; while in the other, you gain. How could preachers say that if it isn't so?"

"I am sure I cannot answer your query as to why preachers have taught you what you say they have taught regarding the date line. But let me say to you and to all, that there is no such thing as gaining or losing time. The expression is unscientific and indicates something that is only apparent, not real.

"Let me illustrate: Two men—twins—start from New York to make the journey around the world. One goes eastward, the other westward. They finally come together again in New York, after a lapse of several months; but he who went eastward finds himself exactly the same age as his brother who traveled the opposite direction. They compare figures, and find that it took each of them the same number of days, hours, and minutes to make the trip, though one added a day and the other dropped a day.

"Now, if it is actually true that one gained and the

other lost a day, there must have been two days' difference in their ages at the journey's end." A ripple of laughter went through the audience. "And if they had repeated the process a sufficient number of times, there would have come a time when one would be old enough to be the other's father." At this the listeners laughed even longer.

"You all see how ludicrous the matter appears when analyzed but a little. The truth is, the whole question is one not of gaining or losing time, but of computation.

"I carry with me," said the captain, "an extract from an article on the date line which I found many years ago, and which, with your permission, I will read. It states the whole proposition more clearly than any word of mine could possibly do. Here it is:

" 'The revolutions of the earth itself, as measured at fixed localities, are what measure and number the days, not the revolutions that may be indicated in the diary of a traveler. A person traveling east or west around the world puts himself at variance with the numerical order of its revolutions as computed at any fixed point; and that variance must be corrected, and that is all the question there is involved in keeping a definite and identical day on a round earth. Attending to this one point, a person need never lose the definite day.

" 'To illustrate: Let us suppose a man to start from some point which we call A, and travel eastward. Suppose he is able to fly around the world, and come back to his starting point, in ten days. Every day, of course, he is carried around by the revolution of the earth. But traveling, as he is, *with* the earth, from west to east, he each day gains upon it one tenth of its circumference; and in ten days, he would gain ten tenths, or a whole circumference. Thus when he arrives at A, he finds that those who have remained there have marked ten revolutions of the earth, and have had ten days of time. But the earth has taken him around as many times as it has them; and in addition to that, he has passed around once himself, which is the same as another revolution for him, making eleven, and giving him, according to his calendar, as he has kept it from day to day, eleven days instead of ten. What shall he do with that extra day?—Drop it out of the count. Why?—Because he knows that the earth itself has made but ten revolutions, as marked at A; and the revolutions of the earth abstractly considered, not the times he may go around it, mark the days, and he must make his count correspond to that of the earth wherever he is.

" 'If the person goes around the earth westward, this process is simply reversed. If he travels at the same rate, his journey each day cancels, or causes him to lose, so far as his count is concerned, one tenth of a revolution of the earth. In ten days, he would lose a whole revolution, and would find, when he came around to his starting point at A, that his calendar showed but nine days instead of ten. What should he do?—Add into his account that lost day. Why?—Because he knows that the earth has made ten revolutions. Although he has himself, like the other man, been around the earth once, it has been in such a direction as apparently to cancel one of its revolutions, and take it out of the count, instead of adding one, as in the other case; and now he must add it in, to be in harmony with the real condition of things.

" 'A common illustration, which may be observed almost any day, may serve to make it a little clearer to the minds of some. Think of a freight train a quarter of a mile in length. It starts, and moves along slowly the distance of its own length, or a quarter of a mile, bringing the rear of the train, when it stops, to the same place where the head of the train stood when it started. Suppose now that a brakeman started from the rear of the train, when the train started, and walked along the cars toward the front, his rate of motion being the same as that of the train itself. When the train stops, he has reached the head of the train, so that although the train has carried him but a quarter of a mile, he has walked another quarter, and so is, in space, half a mile from where he started. But suppose another brakeman, when the train begins to move, starts from the head of the train, and walks toward the rear at the same rate of motion. When the train stops, he has reached the rear. But his motion, being opposite to that of the train, has just balanced, or canceled, for him, the motion of the train; so he finds himself, in space, or compared with surrounding objects, just where he was when the train started. Thus brakeman No. 1 walks a quarter of a mile, doubles the movement of the train, and finds himself, at last, half a mile from the place where he started; and brakeman No. 2 also walks a quarter of a mile, but his motion cancels the movement of the train, and he finds himself at last just where he was in the beginning. On the same principle it is that one going around the earth eastward adds a day to his reckoning, while one going around westward loses a day out of his.' "

Mr. Severance, the merchant, now asked the privilege of supplementing Captain Mann's extract by one which he had preserved. He read as follows:

" 'The reason for this [the adding or dropping of a day at the date line] will be apparent upon a little careful thought; for it is always sunset at some point on the earth, and always sunrise, and noon, and midnight, at other points at the same time. Let us imagine that we could travel around the earth as rapidly as the earth revolves upon its axis, and we start out from London, or from any other place, at sunrise on Tuesday morning, and travel west. It would remain sunrise of the same day with us all the time. Yet when we came to the starting place, we should have to call it the next day; for those who remained there would have had noon, sunset, midnight, and now would have their second morning, which would be Wednesday. Therefore we must change our reckoning, so that at that instant, in any place east of London, we would call it Tuesday morning; but at any point west of that line, it would be Wednesday. That would be the place where the day would change. But for convenience, men have chosen a line that passes through no habitable country, and have fixed that point as a place where the day would change.

" 'By this arrangement, each day is measured off by one revolution of the earth; and when it is finished, it is discharged from the calendar, and a new one takes its place at this point. Hence, wherever we may be on the face of the earth, the day comes to us with its full measure of twenty-four hours, and then is succeeded by another of exactly equal length. It is true that by our traveling east or west, the length of the day may to us be varied; but at the date line, these variations are all rectified. In circumnavigating the globe, we find that we have done so without disarranging our calendar.' "

"Say, captain, who fixed up this date line scheme? And, say, was it agreed to peacefully?" The speaker was a rough-and-ready man from the Western plains, as jovial as he was rough.

"Our friend has suggested a good thought, Captain Mann; so please tell us something of the date line history," said Mr. Severance.

"The date line is a natural result of the order of the peopling of the earth. Taking my Bible, I discover that the cradle of the human family, after the Deluge, was in the valley of the Euphrates, in the Eastern Hemisphere. From that point, people went eastward and westward to the farthest parts of Europe and Africa, and centuries later, still farther west, across the Western Hemisphere. The day originally known in the Euphrates Valley was carried unchanged both east and west, the only difference being that as they went east, they began it earlier, while as they went west, they began it later.

"That this is true is easily seen from the fact that a man may begin a journey in China, and travel westward to San Francisco, and all the way around will find his computation in perfect agreement with the time of the places through which he passes. In other words, he is following the natural route of the day, and thus need make no change. If, however, he goes east from China to San Francisco, he passes the natural starting point, and likewise the finishing point, of the day, and must adjust himself to what he finds."

"Doesn't it bother you at all about keeping Sunday, captain?" asked the friend who sat near him.

"Not in the least, sir," was the reply. "It aids me in my keeping of Sunday, as it aids everyone who is conscientiously seeking to obey God's commandments."

"Say, captain, I'm not a Christian, and don't keep any day, you see; but ever since I was a boy, I have wondered about this Sabbath matter, which the preachers were arguing yesterday," one of the listeners said. "I can understand about the date line now, but I want to know if you honestly think people keep God's commandment when they keep Sunday. Is Sunday the seventh day of the week? I could almost believe it is, if you would tell me so. What do you say, captain? What is your opinion?"

The simplicity and sincerity of the questioner awakened in the captain a tremendous desire to confess what he was rapidly coming to see; namely, that the fourth commandment was not fulfilled in the observance of Sunday. But just as the truth was about to escape his lips, he checked himself. Perhaps the time was not opportune, he thought. With a gracious smile, he therefore said: "Let us refer the theological questions, my dear sir, to the clergy. They will gladly help in such matters."

Harold Wilson, who was standing near Mr. Severance, whispered a word in the merchant's ear.

Mr. Severance was a largehearted, liberal-minded man of affairs; and, acting upon Harold's suggestion, he arose and said:

"Ladies and gentlemen, we have with us on our vessel a Christian gentleman, a man of the cloth, one of deep learning and piety, and to my mind, an authority on this question of the Sabbath. I have heard him preach and therefore feel competent to judge of his ability. I believe we could do no better than to invite Mr. Anderson to give us the privilege of hearing from him in reply to the question we have just heard. All in favor, please raise the hand."

There was an almost unanimous response, though it was noticed that Dr. Spaulding did not vote.

It was arranged that Mr. Anderson should meet his fellow passengers the next day at the same hour.

Mr. Severance created much interest in the meeting of the next day by suggesting that the other clergymen aboard the vessel be present at the service and interrogate the speaker, and thus bring out all phases of the subject.

CHAPTER X

The Strange Preacher Talks

"HE DOESN'T look much like a 'Christ killer,' does he?" whispered one woman to another when, at the appointed hour the next day, Mr. Anderson stood before the passengers in the main parlor.

"Well," replied her friend, "maybe he isn't a Jew; but I've been told, since leaving San Francisco, that he really doesn't believe in Christ. He teaches, so I am informed by one of the ministers aboard our vessel, that we are to be saved by keeping the law rather than by faith in Jesus Christ; and I think that is terrible."

Mr. Anderson smilingly greeted his fellow travelers, assured them that he assumed no superior wisdom, asked them all to be free to contribute of their best thoughts. Laying Harold Wilson's marked Bible on the table before him, he begged that all join him in asking God's Spirit to rest upon their interview and that light might come to all.

What a beautiful, simple prayer he offered! "Our Father who art in heaven," he began, "we thank Thee today for Thy blessed word, which we have met to study.

3—M.B.   (65)

We thank Thee for Jesus, for the great sacrifice He made for us, and that in Him we may find a Friend who is the chiefest among ten thousand, the One altogether lovely. We are thankful for Thy good Spirit, which convinces us of sin, which teaches us the way of life, which reveals Thee, and gives us power to overcome. We hope only in Thy mercy. In us there is no good, and we can come only in that Name which Thou hast caused us to love. Look upon Thine own blessed Son, remember His life, behold us in Him, and know that by faith we make Him just now our personal Redeemer. For all Thy goodness, we praise Thee; and we most earnestly dedicate ourselves to Thee. Direct us at this hour in our study and glorify Thyself in causing us to see a little more fully the truth as it is in Jesus. Amen."

"My!" exclaimed the woman who had just spoken of his supposedly wrong views. "That doesn't sound as I expected. Why, he prays like a Christian! Isn't it strange that one minister should get such a wrong opinion of another?"

"I find," said Mr. Anderson, "that a number of questions have been written and already passed in, and perhaps I ought to notice these first. Is this agreeable?"

Evidently Dr. Spaulding was somewhat fearful, though without reason, that some scheme had been devised to shut out free, open questioning; and having had it in mind to introduce "a few nuts hard to crack," he took occasion to suggest that while the written questions were all right, he should like to have the privilege of introducing at least a few queries first.

Mr. Anderson readily agreed, knowing that courtesy is a principle of the golden rule, which he sought always to follow.

Dr. Spaulding was therefore permitted to have a free

hand. "Do you believe," he began, "that Sabbathkeeping is one of the 'works of the law'?"

"Certainly it is."

"Do you believe that Sabbathkeeping should be regarded as an essential part of our Christian service under the gospel?"

"Most assuredly."

"Very good, brother; and now let me read Paul's words to the Christians of Galatia, and let us see to what your doctrine leads. Galatians 2:16, 21: 'Knowing that a man is not justified by the works of the law, but by the faith of Jesus Christ, even we have believed in Jesus Christ, that we might be justified by the faith of Christ, and not by the works of the law: for by the works of the law shall no flesh be justified.' 'I do not frustrate the grace of God: for if righteousness come by the law, then Christ is dead in vain.'

"Now, if Sabbathkeeping is one of the works mentioned, it frustrates the grace of God and declares that Christ died in vain. That is so, isn't it?"

"Sabbathkeeping," said Mr. Anderson, "is indeed a work of the law, just as any other good deed is also a work. But no one can ever find salvation by performing good works. Christianity knows no such thing as salvation by works. No one can become righteous by any deed of his, however great or good it may seem to be. This is said over and over again in both Romans and Galatians.

"But doing good in order to be saved, or, as Paul states it, to be justified, or made righteous, is altogether different from doing good when through faith one has been saved.

"Works may never truly precede faith and justification, but they as certainly succeed. This must be true;

because before one has through faith found deliverance from sin, it is impossible to do good. The carnal man, with his carnal mind, cannot obey a spiritual law. Romans 8:7. But after sin has been forgiven and the law of the Lord is written in the heart, then all the works of the law appear as naturally as the leaves appear on the trees. In an unconverted life, the works of the law are only dead form; in a converted life, they are the living fruits of the Spirit.

"Sabbathkeeping, therefore, would be only a useless and senseless theory to a person who is not born again, yet one of the covenant experiences to him who has Jesus in the heart."

"Mr. Anderson," said one of the San Francisco women, "you don't believe, then, that people must keep the law as a means of salvation?"

"No, madam; Jesus Christ alone, by our faith, cleanses and saves, and puts Himself within the heart. However, as soon as we have received Him into the life, there are immediately fulfilled in us all the glorious things that the law ordains. See Romans 8:3, 4. Thus faith establishes the law in our hearts as the law of our life. Romans 3:31."

"Well, Mr. Anderson, I want to acknowledge that that is a very beautiful truth. I see it plainly," said the woman. "But may I ask if you really find the Sabbath a blessing —that is, the seventh-day Sabbath? You probably know we have been taught that it is Jewish, a matter of bondage, a yoke which no one can wear with pleasure."

"This reminds me," said Mr. Anderson, "of one of the questions I have in hand here. It reads: 'Why do you not preach Christ instead of so much Sabbath? Is not the preaching of Christ the all-important thing?' Perhaps I may answer the two questions together.

"I wonder if we actually understand the expressions 'preaching the Sabbath' and 'preaching Christ.' What is the Sabbath? Who is Christ?

"To determine the character of the Sabbath, it is necessary to look back to the beginnings of time, to those days before sin came. There we find God's perfect plan. There we see what should have been always, and what will be when the reign of sin is ended.

"The story is that God's work was completed, and all was 'very good.' 'The heavens and the earth were finished, and all the host of them.' Then God rested. 'He rested on the seventh day from all His work which He had made.' Genesis 2:2. In the Paradise home, that home resplendent with the glories of the better world, the great Author of life kept Sabbath with the two beautiful beings who were to have dominion over the earth. And while His created beings kept Sabbath, the heavenly chorus 'sang together, and all the sons of God shouted for joy.' Job 38:7. Surely that first Sabbath must have been a delightsome day, and its service glorious beyond description."

"But, my brother," interrupted Dr. Spaulding, "you would not have this people believe that God was tired, would you?"

"No, and I was intending to cover the point you have made. Let me do so now.

"The Sabbath was not originated nor given to man because of weariness on the part of either God or man. Of the Creator, it is written that He 'fainteth not, neither is weary' (Isaiah 40:28); and man, who was 'in His image,' knew nothing of physical deterioration and decay until after the seeds of sin had been sown. If sin had never entered the world, there would have been no such things as tired nerves or tired muscles, no breaking down of the tissues of life, no sickness, no death. Therefore, as the Sabbath was given before the Fall, its great and primary purpose was not that man should merely cease from his regular employment, but that he should enjoy the same 'rest' the Maker of the world Himself enjoyed.

"Keep this in mind, dear friends, for it is vital to an understanding of the whole matter. He who sees in Sabbathkeeping nothing more than the laying aside of his secular labor for a certain twenty-four hours, and the enjoyment of the privileges of rest, change, and church-going, has not yet found the secret of the Sabbath as it was given to mankind.

"As we have just read, He who made heaven and earth never wearies. He is the great I AM, the Self-existent One, who inhabits eternity, with whom years are not. Yet we read that He rested. More than this, the Bible tells us that 'He rested, and was refreshed.' Exodus 31:17. His was the rest of a divine joy in beholding the perfection of His wonderful handiwork and in receiving from His earth children the love and adoration that sprang from their quick-pulsing and worshipful hearts. It was the rest of communion, of reciprocal affection, of heart understanding. And I believe that I have often found, in my Sabbathkeeping, a little fragment of the restful joy and the joyful rest of that first Eden day when God rested and worshiped with man. It is this beautiful experience that I wish you all to know."

There were some who dared to say, "Amen," and many present found their hearts strangely stirred by the minister's words.

"But let me continue," he said. "That the blessedness of that first Sabbath might be perpetuated, that its experiences might be multiplied and known eternally by all who should live upon earth, God arranged that each succeeding Sabbath should be a repetition of the first. The record is, 'God blessed the seventh day, and sanctified it'—a statement which carries in it the very fullness of divine purpose, divine power, divine presence and wisdom.

"Please note, first, that the Bible text speaks of the *seventh* day; second, that it declares this day is 'sanctified' —that is, set apart or appointed to holy or sacred use. It is the seventh day, not a seventh part of time, that is brought to view."

"May I ask, brother," said Mr. Gregory, "what evidence you have that the first seventh day is now to be identified with Saturday? To my mind, there is much to show that our Sunday is the original seventh day."

"The evidence, Mr. Gregory, is so simple, and withal so complete, that there can scarcely be a mistake. Without question, the fourth commandment calls attention to the seventh day known at the beginning, does it not?"

"I agree with you that far," said Mr. Gregory.

"Very well; and I presume you will also agree with me in holding that the Sabbath kept by the Saviour was the same as that given at Sinai."

"Yes, I think so," was the reply.

"I was sure you would," said Mr. Anderson; "and now let me call your attention to the statement made in Luke 23:56, that, after the crucifixion, the women who had been the most devoted disciples of Christ kept the Sabbath day 'according to the commandment.'"

"Yes; but right there is a missing link. That may have been the ceremonial sabbath of the Passover week rather than the moral Sabbath of the fourth commandment. You see, we must keep track of the week and make sure that we are keeping in touch with the cycle of seven days, which continued unbroken from creation until now."

"That is important, Mr. Gregory, and so important that our Lord has given it emphasis. Let me ask a question: Was the Sabbath that the women kept, the day which came just before that other day, called the 'first day'?"

"Yes, sir, it must have been."

"Another question: Was not that next day the day of the resurrection?"

"It certainly was."

"Then what 'first' day was it? Why, the scripture distinctly states that it was 'the first day of the week.' Do you think, friends, there is any missing link in the connections? I do not believe that even Mr. Gregory will have any question about it. As you see, there is the Sabbath of the fourth commandment, followed by the first day of the week, the week which we all know to be our week of the present time. So we know that the Sabbath of the fourth commandment, which is the Sabbath of creation, is the seventh day of our week. It is therefore the day which we are to observe and in which we shall find blessing. Isn't that plain?"

There was no dissent. Mr. Anderson had carried his audience with him.

"And do you remember the story of the burning bush? Exodus 3:1-6. God's presence was revealed to Moses; and the word came, 'Put off thy shoes from off thy feet, for the place whereon thou standest is holy.' The presence of God made the very surroundings holy. The same word was spoken to Joshua. Joshua 5:13-15.

"Thus we learn this: God's blessing is His own presence. His presence imparted to man makes the man holy; His presence manifested in a place makes the place holy. The rest of the story is plain—His presence, His blessing, in the seventh day makes the seventh day holy.

"When God blessed the seventh day, He simply put His presence into that day for all earth's history. He did this for man. You know that Jesus said, 'The Sabbath was made for man.' And how wonderful, then, was the making! Every seventh day brings His blessed, holy presence. The holy day carries its sanctifying, cleansing, uplifting power into the heart of God's worshiping ones, and makes them glad in the gift of holiness.

"The Author of the Sabbath was Jesus Christ. Read John 1:1-3, 14; Colossians 1:13-16. It is His presence which the seventh day incloses. It is His life of which I partake in Sabbathkeeping. And do I not therefore preach Him when I truly preach the Sabbath? Ah, this Sabbath truth is among the grandest of all the grand things brought to view in the word of God!"

"Amen!" called out Harold Wilson, who, by special invitation of Captain Mann, was present; and all eyes turned his way.

Captain Mann was visibly affected. He recognized a witnessing voice that was speaking to his soul. It was the voice of truth, which he could not reject.

Dr. Spaulding and Mr. Gregory quietly waited until Mr. Anderson had offered a short prayer, then they left.

"Spaulding, what did you think of that?" asked Mr. Gregory when they were alone.

CHAPTER XI

Interested Questioners

"MR. ANDERSON, you will pardon me, I am sure, if I detain you a few moments. This service has simply compelled me to come and take you by the hand, and to express to you my appreciation."

Mr. Anderson did not recognize the man.

"Of course, you do not know me; and may I therefore introduce myself as Judge Kershaw of Little Rock, Arkansas?"

"Oh, and you are the man who interrogated Dr. Spaulding yesterday?"

"Yes, sir, though perhaps I should be ashamed of what has since appeared to me an impertinence. But, you see, Dr. Spaulding's statements greatly stirred me, as I remembered the occasion of several years ago, when, at his instance, a member of your denomination was brought before me for Sunday violation."

A group of interested passengers began to form as soon as Judge Kershaw began to speak. Harold Wilson was among them.

"At that time," the judge continued, "I thought I discovered on the part of the prosecution a distinct spirit of intolerance, which to my mind is utterly foreign to the gospel of Jesus Christ. But while this was true, the young defendant manifested most beautiful patience and self-restraint; and as he acted as his own counsel, I was persuaded that his principles were of a high order."

"Was he convicted, judge?" asked one of the listeners.

"Yes; the letter of the law had been violated, the jury brought in a verdict of guilty, and I was obliged to pass sentence. But I was hurt, deeply hurt—hurt in one sense by the wrong spirit shown by the professed Christians who prosecuted, and hurt in another sense by the excellent spirit of the one who was condemned.

"Now I believe I have discovered the secret of that young man's behavior. He had Christ in his soul. He had a rest and peace to which all of us were strangers. Why, when I was about to pass sentence and asked him if he had any further word to give the court, he said: 'Your Honor, I wish to thank you and the gentlemen of the jury for the spirit of fairness shown during the trial. You need have no regret that you are obliged to pass this sentence. We may all well be sad that our statute books are cumbered with a few laws that work hardship to innocent and inoffensive citizens, and personally I hope to see the day come when our fair state will abolish this particular law which today sends me to prison. I submit gladly to the penalty, as a Christian ought. I forgive freely the men who have brought me this experience. And I want you all to know that in my heart there is a peace passing all understanding, a peace which will brighten every day and hour I shall spend behind the bars.'

"I sent him to prison, and in the prison he died. And from that day until now, I have had his picture much before me, and I have wanted to know what it was that made him the man he was."

"Judge, pardon me; but I, too, have found the peace which the young man had," said Harold Wilson, "and I have found it since coming aboard the vessel. I have found it in this Sabbath truth which was presented today."

"Young man, I do not doubt you. You are the one, are you not, who is called 'the man with the marked Bible'?"

"Yes, sir; and I asked Mr. Anderson to read from my marked Bible today."

Judge Kershaw picked up the Book and glanced through it. There was moisture in his eyes.

"Mr. Anderson," he said, "this reminds me of my boyhood, when my parents sought to lead me to a religious life. Like many boys, I was foolishly inclined to make light of Christianity; and ere I could realize it, my youthful days had passed, and I found myself graduated from college and entering upon my professional career without a hope. My education only served to crystallize my early unbelief; and all through the years since, I have seen little or nothing in the average church or its teachings to cause me to change.

"One thought, however, has always followed me—a thought expressed by my mother. A few days before she died, she called me to her and said: 'Son, I know I have not always lived before you as I should, and you have your doubts about Christianity. But some day, I know not when, you will surely see that God's word is true, that there are those who have proved it divine; and thus you will be led to yield your heart to the Author, and love and serve Him.' You will not know, unless I tell you, why this Bible reminds me of those times so long ago. Well, it is marked as mother marked hers. And, strange to say, the Ten Commandments were specially remembered, even as in this. Mother was a firm believer in every one of the commandments of God.

"But think of it! Here I am, an old man of seventy years. It is nearly time for me to go. Do you suppose this is the hour when mother's prayer should be answered?"

There was a period of deep silence. All seemed to realize that a sacred decision was being made, a decision involving the salvation of a soul, in answer to a prayer offered by a devoted mother a half century before.

Now Mr. Severance spoke: "Judge, this day has been a day of revelation to me also. But I must know more. Mr. Anderson, may I ask you a few brief questions? For instance, if the seventh day is the Sabbath day, and if we are morally bound to make it our day of rest, why does the church as a whole not see and acknowledge it? This troubles me."

"I have no doubt, Mr. Severance," Mr. Anderson began, "that there are many causes which have led the professed Christian world to observe Sunday rather than Sabbath. However, I may venture the remark that the Sabbath has been set aside for the same reason that other great moral duties have been neglected or rejected. You will remember that the apostle Paul clearly foretold a time when professed Christians would 'not endure sound doctrine,' but would 'heap to themselves teachers, having itching ears,' and would 'turn away their ears from the truth.' 2 Timothy 4:3, 4.

"A brief examination of the word of God shows that this evil course has been common all through the ages.

"It has always been apparently easy for men to estimate lightly the word of God. Surely it is so now, when higher criticism finds ready access to both pulpit and pew, placing the writings of Inspiration on the same level as the works of Shakespeare, Emerson, Spenser, and others. The day has come when even the Ten Commandments are regarded by many as out of date and in need of revision."

"Yes," said one of those in the group, "I was told only yesterday, by a man who looked like a minister, that we can no longer hold the Bible as an absolutely unquestioned authority. He said that much of the Old Testament had been shown to be unhistorical, and that the miracles recorded in the Gospels were largely allegorical. I asked him particularly about the resurrection and ascension of Christ, and he only shrugged his shoulders and smiled."

"Of course, Mr. Severance," continued Mr. Anderson, "not all the professed people of God have so far departed from the old paths that they have thus set the Scriptures aside. There are many beautiful and notable exceptions. But if you would know why the churches of today, generally speaking, reject the Sabbath truth, you will find the reason in the facts I have pointed out."

"Mr. Anderson," said Judge Kershaw, "what you have given us from the prophetic Scriptures is being strikingly fulfilled at this very time. I have just completed the reading of a magazine article entitled, 'Blasting at the Rock of Ages,' which shows that all through our advanced institutions of learning, including our theological seminaries, open infidelity is taught. Positions are taken which completely nullify every moral principle contained in the word of God. I could hardly believe my eyes. And these are the schools from which, of course, our ministers are sent forth."

"I am not in the least disposed to criticize," Mr. Anderson responded, "for criticism is a dangerous practice. But you must know, for your own soul's sake, the dangers of this time, and kindly warn against them. For instance, you have heard it said that truth cannot be known, and that the Bible, like a violin, plays whatever tune is desired, and that this is God's plan. The statement is frequently made, that 'the truth of today is the error of tomorrow,' and *vice versa*. But Jesus said, 'Ye shall know the truth' (John 8:32), and, 'If any man will do His will, he shall know of the doctrine' (John 7:17). When a man hungers and thirsts for truth, the Holy Spirit reveals to him the deep things of God, and makes them a part of his very life. Read 1 Corinthians 2:9-12. See also John 6:45; 16:13-15.

"Again, you will hear it taught that if you are 'only sincere' in what you do, your service is accepted. This sounds good, but it is misleading. Sincerity is necessary, but it never excuses ignorance."

"Now let me understand you, Mr. Anderson," said Mr. Severance. "Has not my sincere observance of Sunday been acknowledged of God? I have surely tried to be a Christian."

"Yes, brother, you have undoubtedly enjoyed God's love, because you gladly did all you knew to be right. But suppose you see the truth of the fourth commandment and then fail to follow it. Jesus said regarding those in His day, 'If I had not come and spoken unto them, they had not had sin: but now they have no cloak for their sin.' John 15:22. Paul pointed out the same principle when he said, 'The times of this ignorance God winked at; but now commandeth all men everywhere to repent.' Acts 17:30. Sincerity in wrongdoing ceases to be possible when the light reveals the better way. Sincerity then obliges a man to change his course."

Harold Wilson, intensely enthusiastic in his new-found experience and eager to learn, asked the privilege of another question.

"Mr. Anderson, one of the ministers has told me that it is all right to keep the seventh day, but the only question is, Where shall we begin to count? He said he kept the seventh day, but he began his count on Monday. What do you think about it?"

"That is what I have been taught," said Mr. Severance.

"I have already partially answered the question, but let us notice it further.

"Turn to Exodus 16 and the story of the manna. God said He wanted to 'prove' or 'try' the people, as to whether they would walk in His law. The plan was that the people should gather their food every day from the first to the sixth. Each day for five days, they were to gather only as much as they needed for that day, planning to have nothing remain over until the morning. On the sixth day, however, they were to gather a supply for two days, the second portion being for use on the seventh day, when no manna fell. This was the Lord's arrangement.

"Now, the count of the days was not left to man's choice. God Himself did the numbering. And if anyone, purposely or otherwise, tried to make a change, and did not accommodate himself to God's order, there resulted only confusion and loss, besides definite reproof from the Lord. Evidently some attempted a change by trying to keep the food over until morning; but 'it bred worms, and stank.' Verse 20. Others went out on the seventh day to gather manna (possibly because they failed to secure the double portion of the sixth day), but found none. (Verse 27.) It was absolutely impossible to change the count.

"Now note the message which came as a result of their

careless disobedience: 'How long refuse ye to keep My commandments and My laws?' Verse 28. The test of loyalty was upon the matter of right counting—counting as God counted, with the Sabbath as the great objective.

"It may be of interest to you to know that in early days, the Hebrew people were accustomed to relate each day of the week to the Sabbath by a very unusual method: they named the days as 'First into the Sabbath,' 'Second into the Sabbath,' and so on through the entire week. The Sabbath was really counted every day. And never forget that by three miracles every week, God pointed out the particular and absolute seventh day of the week: first by granting a double portion of manna on the sixth day; second by withholding it altogether on the seventh day; and third by preserving the extra portion on the seventh day."

"Well, Mr. Anderson, that certainly settles the question of the count. Still, it isn't altogether clear to me just why the absolute day is so necessary." The speaker was Mr. Severance.

"A simple illustration, I believe, will make this clear. Let me place before you seven glasses. Six are filled with water, one with rare and delicious fruit nectar. I say to you, If you will take the seventh glass, you will find one of the most delightful beverages ever known. You desire the thing of which I speak. Yet there is only one glass containing it, only one glass that is 'the seventh' glass, and you must take my count to find what you are after. If I may state it thus, the blessing of the fruit nectar is wrapped up in my numbering of the glasses.

"Just so it is with the Sabbath. God blessed the seventh day. He put His presence into that particular day and into no other. And if I find Him as my heart really longs to know Him, I must begin to count as He counted, making my first, second, third, fourth, fifth, sixth, and seventh correspond to His. And when I do so, I am rewarded by actually finding Him, knowing Him, resting in Him. Because I am with Him in the Sabbath, I have rest. The true and intelligent Sabbathkeeper, therefore, has in his service a blessing that not even a sincere Sundaykeeper ever knows."

"I see it, Mr. Anderson, I see it," declared Mr. Severance; "and this day I join you in the larger service of the Sabbath that God has given. Will you pray for me? I especially need help in arranging my business."

"I praise the dear Lord, Mr. Severance, for this decision. It is the decision of faith, I am sure. God will help you in shaping your affairs for His service."

"I have in mind, however," said Mr. Severance, "more than you think. This is a day of tremendous conviction. My business career all through the years has been along lines that the world may regard as legitimate; but something has told me this afternoon that if I would be holy, and know Him who is holy, and enjoy Him in His holy day, I must retrace many of my steps. I must adjust all my methods to different standards, and go before my patrons and business associates in confession. Yes, even more, I shall have to let many a dollar revert to its real owner. Do you believe God will enable me to bear the cross?"

At this juncture, Captain Mann entered the room.

CHAPTER XII

A Sabbath Rescue From Drowning

AT THE close of Mr. Anderson's service in the parlor, Dr. Spaulding, in company with Mr. Gregory, had sought a quiet place on deck to discuss what had been said and done. They were both much agitated, though the latter was inclined to acknowledge the truth of many things he had heard.

But while they talked together, Captain Mann passed near. Dr. Spaulding called to him.

"Captain, just a moment of your time. I simply want to make an appeal. Can we not devise some plan to stop further spread of this Sabbath talk? It is not producing the best results, inasmuch as it stirs up the spirit of unwholesome argument and sooner or later may be the means of unsettling the views of some very good Christian people who are aboard. That young man with the marked Bible is already completely misled, and I notice that he is influencing others. You see, captain, I am terribly afraid of fanaticism."

"Well, Dr. Spaulding, you are aware that you are at liberty to plan as you wish. The freedom of the vessel is yours. But let me say to you, in the brief moment that I may stop, that the young man of whom you speak, Harold Wilson, has become, during the brief period since we left San Francisco, such a splendid Christian, such a trustworthy and capable co-worker, that I marvel. From a profligate, a drinking, swearing, gambling, thieving criminal, as I have known him, he has been transformed into the sober, praying, industrious, honest young man you behold today. This certainly must be the fruit of a good tree. And I confess that I myself have tasted and been made better.

"I must hasten; but let me assure you that this is something of which you need not be afraid. It is not fanaticism. There is a large amount of zeal, but it is founded on knowledge of the Bible. No one can go far astray who studies the word of God in order to live. And Harold Wilson is living it."

The captain passed quickly on and into the parlor.

The view that met his eye as he entered was one which he was never to forget. There sat Mr. Severance, bowed over the table, with face buried in hands. And as he entered, Harold Wilson, Bible in hand and with his arm thrown over the shoulder of the merchant, was bearing witness to him of the surety of God's promise and of the wonderful blessing that had come to him in the truth of the fourth commandment.

As Captain Mann beheld the spirit manifested by Harold—the spirit of the real soul winner and helper of those in trouble—his emotions overcame him, and tears filled his eyes. How strange, yet how beautiful, was this expression of tenderness in this hardy veteran of the sea!

But not a word escaped his lips. He simply stepped

over to Mr. Anderson, gripped his hand strongly and feelingly, and with quivering lip hastened on to his duty.

A shriek startled the little group in the dining room, and almost immediately the cry, "Woman overboard!" began to sound from one end of the vessel to the other.

"Who is it? Who is it?" was on everyone's tongue. But no one knew.

The two clergymen—Dr. Spaulding and Mr. Gregory —rushed to the opposite side of the vessel, reaching the rail just in time to see Harold Wilson emerge from the main parlor, quickly lay down his Bible, take off his coat, and plunge into the sea.

"Ah, how foolish! How foolish!" exclaimed Dr. Spaulding. "It means two lives instead of one. No living man can handle himself in the wake of this vessel."

"But God help him!" was Mr. Gregory's response.

And God surely did help. The brave act of Harold was one of faith; and even while he battled with the waters, his thoughts went up to God for help and deliverance, and his prayer was graciously answered.

His eye caught sight of a hand as it appeared for an instant above the swirling waters a few feet away, and he threw himself toward it with all the might at his command.

The drowning woman's dress was now in his hand, and quickly and deftly he made sure of his human treasure and started toward the vessel.

"Thank God!" called out Dr. Spaulding. The passengers cheered and wept.

Meanwhile Captain Mann had ordered the engines reversed, and the great "Pacific Clipper" was brought to a dead stop, a lifeboat was lowered, and Harold and the yet unknown woman were soon safely lifted to the deck.

Mr. Gregory pressed his way to the center of the scene,

that he might grasp the hand of the young hero, and incidentally be of whatever service possible. But as he was about to reach for Harold's hand, the face of the rescued woman, now partially resuscitated, was before him.

His face blanched, his strength gave way, and he fell heavily to the deck. It was his wife!

"Mr. Wilson," said Mrs. Gregory, as she lay in her stateroom the next day, "I must tell you why I have sent for you. My husband here must know also.

"I was at the service yesterday in the parlor and heard Mr. Anderson discuss the Sabbath question; and while I am ashamed to say it, I was really angry at some things that were said. I didn't like to hear them, and I didn't want others to hear. And, of course, I blamed you. Someone had told me that it was because of your relations with Mr. Anderson that the service was held; and when, at the last, I heard you say, 'Amen,' I said to myself, 'I wish that young upstart would fall overboard, and thus deliver us from any more Sabbath talk.'

"After the meeting, I came to my room and tried to forget the whole thing; but I couldn't, so I returned after a time. As I saw you still there, I was more bitter than ever. I passed the parlor door; but as I did so, my feelings overcame me. I grew dizzy (I have such spells when my feelings run away with me), and—well, I knew no more until I awakened on deck and learned that I had been delivered from a watery grave. And you, the object of my evil wishes, were chosen of God to be my rescuer!

"Mr. Wilson, I am begging your forgiveness, which I am sure you will give; but I am begging more—I am going to ask you to take your Bible and tell me more about the truth which I have been trying to reject."

Harold humbly acknowledged his great ignorance and asked if she would not rather study with Mr. Anderson.

"Do you think he would be willing to come?" she asked.

"Oh, I am sure he would!" was the reply. And Harold hastened to bring his friend.

"Mr. Anderson," said Mrs. Gregory, "I am deeply in earnest today, and husband and I both desire further instruction. The terrible happening of yesterday was from God, to correct us and make us willing to receive unadulterated teaching. Now, what I want to ask is, Why do you specially emphasize the question of the seventh-day Sabbath? Does God require you to do it? And why is it that so many people, especially the ministers, are so determined not to listen to your message?"

"Sister, your questions are rather broad, and really require more study than the circumstances will permit. However, they are to the point, and I am glad the Scriptures can give you an answer.

"Let me call your attention first to the fact that along with marriage, the Sabbath is one of the great blessings that have come down to us from the Eden home. Marriage was designed to preserve a sacred relationship between members of the human family; the Sabbath, to preserve a sacred relationship between the human family and the Creator.

"The most casual reading of the fourth commandment shows the great purpose of the Sabbath. 'Remember the Sabbath day, to keep it holy. . . . For in six days the Lord made heaven and earth.' Exodus 20:8-11. The Sabbath was to help men keep in mind the making of the heaven and the earth. It is the memorial of that great work. It keeps before the mind God's creative power. It calls upon us to obey Him because He is Creator, and, in its service, bequeaths to us the power necessary to overcome. True Sabbathkeeping means constant surrender to God and, therefore, has always been the one thing that has kept man from idolatry.

"This is beautifully brought out in the words of Exodus 31:17: 'It is a sign between Me and the children of Israel forever.' And Ezekiel tells us, 'I [the Lord] gave them My Sabbaths, to be a sign between Me and them, that they might know that I am the Lord that sanctify them.' Ezekiel 20:12, 20. The reason is that God, or Christ, puts Himself, His own presence, into the day, and through its acceptance, into the Sabbathkeeper's heart. Thus every Sabbath renews and strengthens faith in the Creator.

"You will note that the Sabbath is a sign between God and Israel *forever*. This does not refer only to Jews, the mere fleshly descendants of Abraham, for they soon gave up real Sabbathkeeping, and therefore did not know the Sabbath as a blessing. 'Israel' means more than Jews. The term is one that includes the true believer in all ages, and down to the end of time. All Christians are spiritual Israelites. See Romans 2:28, 29; John 1:47; Galatians 3:29. Hence all who would be kept in the way of righteousness will keep Sabbath, and find it a sign, a memorial, of His redeeming power. Creation and redemption, you see, are the same, both calling for the Sabbath memorial."

"Yes, I can see that," said Mrs. Gregory. "Isn't it beautiful!"

"With this thought in mind, it is very easy to see why the Lord has always emphasized the truth of the Sabbath. As you remember, it was the test that God brought to Israel in Egypt (Exodus 5:5); it was the test thirty days before they came to Sinai (Exodus 16); and at Sinai, the fourth commandment was specially revealed. Nehemiah 9:14. All the commandments were important—this goes without saying; but only the Sabbath is He said to have made 'known.' The Sabbath is peculiarly vital.

"Listen also to the striking word of Isaiah, the gospel prophet: 'If thou turn away thy foot from the Sabbath, from doing thy pleasure on My holy day; and call the Sabbath a delight, the holy of the Lord, honorable; and shalt honor Him: . . . then shalt thou delight thyself in the Lord; and I will cause thee to ride upon the high places of the earth.' Isaiah 58:13, 14. How plain the prophet makes it, doesn't he, that all spiritual power and uplift are to be found in the Sabbath of God!

"I have said that Isaiah is 'the gospel prophet.' He is. This which we have read has reference to our own gospel time. God is calling, in Isaiah's message, for us to turn our feet from the Sabbath, to stop trampling it underfoot. And the promise is actually fulfilled to those who obey."

"Mr. Anderson, Harold Wilson impresses me as having found a great blessing," said Mr. Gregory.

"Yes, and in this very truth. He has kept only one Sabbath, but he found a remarkable blessing in it. Really, dear people, it was what came into his soul from the Sabbath, that carried him over the ship's side yesterday. He has told me this. And he is certain that God regarded his obedience, and answered his prayer in his finding you. He calls you his 'Sabbath-saved woman.'"

"I don't doubt it, not for a moment," Mrs. Gregory replied; "and that is why I am really and truly opening my heart today."

"But let me continue a bit further. In the fifty-sixth chapter of his book, Isaiah prophesies of a great Sabbath **reform** among the Gentiles of these last days. Read verses 1-8, and you will see that it is specially a gospel message, and promises those who enter into a Sabbath covenant with Him 'a place and a name better than of sons and of daughters.' He will give them 'an everlasting name, that shall not be cut off.' Everlasting life is involved.

"Surely, then, someone must preach that Sabbath message at this time. Someone must specially emphasize its importance, even as God asks."

"Well, Mr. Anderson, why is it, then, that the ministers—those of other denominations—do not accept these plain statements? They certainly are plain, though I never read them before. But the ministers have read them."

"I can tell you why some of them do not accept," said Mr. Gregory. "They are a little too much as I am. They do not like to acknowledge that they have been wrong. If all the clergymen who really see the truth of this Sabbath question were to confess their convictions, there would be few left to offer opposition. I know whereof I affirm. Scores of them have privately admitted to me that the Sabbatarians are right."

"Well, husband, you have never said that before in my presence. I call that dishonesty."

"Better not say that, wife. Rather look at it as a blindness, which for a time hinders them from reading their own motives," said Mr. Gregory.

"Pardon me, dear friends," said Mr. Anderson. "I have not completed the study, but I am sure you are both weary. The strain of yesterday's experience has told on your strength, and you had better rest. I will therefore go. The Lord quickly restore you to your full strength. Good-by!"

CHAPTER XIII

Meeting God in the Way

"HUSBAND," said Mrs. Gregory, when they were alone in the seclusion of their cabin, "what are you going to do about this truth of the Sabbath?"

A rap announced a "short call" from Dr. Spaulding.

"Mr. Spaulding, I am so glad you came in," said Mrs. Gregory, "for my husband and I have just been talking about a matter of personal duty, and I want to take you into our confidence."

Dr. Spaulding glanced about the stateroom somewhat nervously, instinctively detecting that the matter of "personal duty" was one which, above all others, he would at this time avoid. His distress was apparent, particularly when he saw lying near, Harold Wilson's Bible, which in the young man's haste had been left behind.

"Perhaps you have not long to stay with us," continued Mrs. Gregory, "so I will come at once to my point."

Dr. Spaulding's eyes seemed to be riveted on a Scripture text which, as a motto for the voyage, Mrs. Gregory had pinned to the side wall of the stateroom.

"You see, Dr. Spaulding, husband and I have been

taken through a hard experience. As you know, yesterday God sent me down through 'the valley of the shadow;' and as I consider all the circumstances, I am profoundly convinced that it was to teach me to be willing to bear my cross as the Lord Jesus would have me.

"I have been bitterly opposed to the idea of observing the true Sabbath of the Lord, although ever since I was a child, I have heard something ever telling me that Sunday is not the Christian's day of rest. Yesterday that bitterness nearly cost me my life, and only the heroic act of a Sabbathkeeper saved me. However, I have come to see what God wants me to do, and I mean to do it.

"Husband also sees. He, too, is convinced that the truths spoken yesterday, and at other times also, call for surrender on our part. My question is—and here I am treating you indeed as a confidential friend—Do you not think we should both come out at once and openly take our stand in favor of the Sabbath? You are an ambassador for Christ, and I want you to give me your sincerest thought."

Little did the good woman know that the day before, at the very time she was precipitated into the sea, Dr. Spaulding was seeking to persuade her husband that Harold Wilson was a menace to the Christian belief of a vast majority of the passengers, and that Mr. Anderson was one who should be shunned by both ministers and people.

Mr. Gregory sensed the embarrassment of the situation, and sought to alleviate Spaulding's distress.

"Spaulding," he said, "do you not regard it as remarkable, in view of what we were discussing at the time of the accident, that Mr. Wilson should have been the one to save my wife's life? And mark you, he himself has said that the truth which has recently come to him was

what gave him inspiration and faith to jump overboard
and effect the rescue. Do you not look upon it as remarkable?"

"Yes, Gregory, I do; and I confess myself reproved for
what I said."

"But you must answer my question, Dr. Spaulding,"
Mrs. Gregory insisted. "Do you not think we should
both keep the Sabbath, even though it may cost us everything we have in the world, when we have come to
understand that God is calling upon us to do so?"

"Mrs. Gregory, you have placed me in an exceedingly
trying position, yet you have done so unwittingly. You
may not be aware that I have been strongly opposed to
the seventh-day Sabbath idea and have regarded it as a
delusion, something that is calculated to hinder the
progress of the gospel in this time of great world evan-
gelism. But to be perfectly frank, I will say that it is
everyone's privilege and duty to obey his conscience."

"Spaulding," queried Mr. Gregory, "do you feel absolutely confident that you are right in the positions you
have taken regarding the Sabbath? For instance, are
you ready to stake your salvation on the thought that the
Sabbath is not to be kept, because the law is abolished?
Really, didn't Jesus honor the Ten Commandments and
die to satisfy their claims? Does not the story of Calvary
show that the law of the new covenant, the law written in
the heart, is the law proclaimed from Sinai? Before God,
tell me. Let us be honest with our own hearts."

"Well, Gregory, I don't know how to analyze my position. When I read such texts as Matthew 5:17, 18;
Romans 3:31; 8:3, 4; James 2:8-12; Matthew 19:17, and
other like passages, there does flit through my mind a bit
of doubt. No, I cannot truly say I am absolutely confident."

"Another question, then," continued Mr. Gregory:

"Ought we not to regard the example and teaching of Jesus as vital?"

"Yes, I believe we ought."

Dr. Spaulding began to relax, and a spirit of freedom which he almost unwillingly enjoyed began to take possession of him.

"Well, that is my opinion, too," continued Mr. Gregory. "For a long time, I have had in mind that if I would yield my pride, and freely follow the Saviour's plan, I would be a Sabbathkeeper. He certainly was, yet not as a Jew; Jesus was the Universal Man, and therefore His Sabbathkeeping was of universal import. He is my example, and I see no way to escape the conclusion that I should do as He did.

"You told me, Spaulding, that you had been connected with one of the seminaries conducted by your people, and that you taught church history. Tell me, please, has not your study shown you that the Sabbath of the fourth commandment was kept by the apostles and by the church generally for hundreds of years after Christ? Is it not true that the early church was influenced by the forms and ceremonies of ancient pagan sun worship and that gradually she adopted the customs of the time, Sunday observance being one of them? And, to make a long story short, was it not the church, fallen and corrupted, seeking for worldly position and power, that, in the fourth century, actually substituted Sunday for the Sabbath, and compelled the recognition of it by law?"

"Gregory, you are down to real heart work now," was Dr. Spaulding's reply, "and I am going to be frank. I am going to tell you what I have never breathed to a soul before; namely, that all you have said and even more is true. Without any doubt, Sunday as a day of rest is only a child of apostasy. There is not a snatch of evidence, in any of the writings of the fathers, to prove that it has any claim to divine sanction. I know all this.

"But I have looked at the matter from another angle —I have given respectful consideration to the thought that as Sunday was the day of the resurrection, we could properly celebrate that glorious event by worshiping on the day which witnessed it. I must say, though, that if I were on my dying bed, I should not want to make any strong claim for the practice. Certainly God never commanded it."

"Then tell me, Dr. Spaulding," said Mrs. Gregory, "how in the world could you stand before the people week after week and teach something of which you were not absolutely sure? Don't you believe the Bible?"

"Mrs. Gregory, let me bare my heart a bit further. You have now suggested the real difficulty of the whole proposition. I believe I have been playing with the word of God. I recognize that there has come into my life a something which has undermined my old-time confidence. The Bible has ceased to be a really authoritative Divine Record. I have treated it, in a measure, as though it were from men rather than from the Lord; and on that account, I have argued just to carry my point and not to find the truth."

"I have done the same, to some extent," said Mr. Gregory.

"Well, are you both intending to continue that course?" asked Mrs. Gregory. "It seems to me that God is trying very earnestly here today to help us all to change."

"And become Sabbatarians, Mrs. Gregory?" Dr. Spaulding questioned.

"I didn't say that, yet maybe that is what any true and complete change would mean. You know, Dr. Spaulding, that if we do take God's word as an inspired oracle and as our only guide in living, there is no escaping the fact that we are under absolute moral obligation to obey the fourth commandment. Isn't that so?"

"Certainly," was the answer. "There is not a hint that any other day was divinely set apart."

"So far as the Bible is concerned, then, the Sabbatarians are correct, are they not?"

"Yes, without doubt. But, oh, the idea of keeping a day different from what almost the entire Christian church observes! It is that that hurts me. Why, one actually becomes the laughingstock of society. I myself have called the seventh-day people 'Christ killers' and 'fanatics.'"

"You certainly have, Spaulding," said Mr. Gregory. "Those were the terms you were using yesterday when we were interrupted by the cry, 'Woman overboard!'"

"Well, I never knew before that ministers of the gospel were so unwilling to yield to what they knew to be right. And do you mean to tell me that there are others in the pulpit who talk one thing and believe another?" exclaimed Mrs. Gregory.

"Wife, you must be patient and charitable in this matter, even though you learn of what seems to be dishonesty. I don't like to call it that; rather, I would call it confusion, resulting from long years of training in the wrong direction. As Spaulding has said, he has scarcely been able to analyze his own views. We have gone on, however, teaching many times what we have not known to be true, even though we have not taught what we have known to be false. It is perfectly safe to say that the majority of the ministry of today occupy this position. But the circumstances of this trip,—the contact with Harold Wilson and his marked Bible, the attitude of Captain

Mann, the work of Mr. Anderson, the discussions among Mr. Mitchell, Dr. Spaulding, and me, and finally, the providence of yesterday, which has spoken so pointedly to my soul,—all these have caused me to see that I must take an entirely different course, and I purpose that everyone aboard this vessel shall know what God has done for me." It was thus that Mr. Gregory, led by the Spirit of God, finally and fully committed himself.

"Before you go, Spaulding, won't you take the Bible there and read for us? Read the fortieth psalm, please."

Dr. Spaulding gladly acceded to the request of Mr. Gregory, and, picking up the marked Bible, turned to the psalm indicated and began to read. Slowly and feelingly he read, a great tenderness taking possession of his heart. Scores and scores of times during his ministry he had read this same passage; but never before had its voice seemed to speak so directly to him, or its message appeared so sweet. He reached the eighth verse, and this he found underscored. In the margin was written the following: "God's *will* is God's *law*. To do His will— to keep His law—is the true and only object of life. Ecclesiastes 12:13. Not wealth, not health, not happiness, not salvation, not philanthropy, but doing God's gracious will. He who delights in the will of God has found the climax of all holiness and will surely be instrumental, as Jesus was, in leading others to love and serve. This is the revelation of God in man and through man.—Mother."

Dr. Spaulding stopped. The word "Mother" at the close of the note aroused in him a peculiar interest. He asked, "Who is the mother who wrote this comment?"

While the words were on his lips, there was a light rap at the door. In response to the usual "Come in," Harold Wilson entered. He had missed his Bible, and had come for it.

"Sit down, my boy," said Mr. Gregory. "We are just about to have prayer with Dr. Spaulding."

That sounded strange to Harold; and what was stranger, his Bible was in Dr. Spaulding's hand. What did it mean?

Spaulding soon satisfied Harold's curiosity by explaining the circumstances, and then, in a gentle and fatherly way, so unlike his usual demeanor, said: "Son, what is the meaning of the word 'Mother' signed to this note here? I am interested, because the note sounds so much like the words of my own mother, who was accustomed also to mark her Bible."

Gladly indeed did Harold relate the story of his faithful mother, of his effort to escape her influence and teaching, of the marked Bible which he found at sea and later threw away, of his life in sin, of his trial and sentence, of the marked Bible at the Oakland pier—marked by request of his mother while she was on her deathbed—of Mr. Anderson's acquaintance with the dear mother, and of Captain Mann and his experience. All this and much more seemed to Harold a chapter stranger than fiction, and he told it as only one who believes in an overshadowing Providence can.

"And that's why I am trying to follow my Saviour," said Harold. "My mother's prayer has been answered through Mr. Anderson. The verse you have just read is my special guide, and I wrote my name under the word 'Mother,' so I could say in my heart that I was endorsing her message."

Dr. Spaulding prayed. The Spirit of God was there. As he prayed, his heart broke before God. Mr. and Mrs. Gregory shared fully his blessing of spiritual uplift, and amens sought to find expression through lips too tender to articulate. When he prayed for Harold, "the hero of faith" of the day before, and for Mr. Anderson, "the devoted brother who sought truly to reveal Christ," Harold's cup was full.

The prayer ended, Harold quietly withdrew, and Dr. Spaulding also hastened to his stateroom.

But before the gong called Harold to his work, he went to Mr. Anderson's quarters and told him what had occurred in the stateroom he had just left.

"Thank God," said the minister, "the day of miracles is not past."

CHAPTER XIV

Light From Prophecy

IT WAS Sabbath morning, a bright, beautiful day. Several days had now elapsed since the almost miraculous rescue of Mrs. Gregory; and Harold Wilson had frequently been stopped here and there by interested persons who desired to ask him about his conversion, his marked Bible, and his answered prayer in the saving of the minister's wife.

Besides the interest shown in the young man, there were rumors afloat that one of the clergymen had "become a seventh-day man." But no one seemed to know whether it was Mr. Mitchell, Dr. Spaulding, or Mr. Gregory.

Until this Sabbath morning, no one had given particular attention to a certain man, evidently educated and cultured, who had kept himself somewhat isolated. He attended none of the religious services aboard the vessel, but spent much time reading some well-worn books that he carried with him.

Determined that the journey should not end before he had at least made an effort at acquaintance, Mr. Anderson, finding him at his accustomed reading, took a seat beside him on deck, and as his custom was, inquired if the man was a Christian.

"Yes, sir; I am a Roman Catholic, a member of the

(100)

only true and apostolic church," the stranger said, very positively.

"Ah! Well, I am glad to meet you, sir," was the minister's reply. "I am a Protestant; but that does not hinder me from feeling brotherly."

"Do you say you are a Protestant? There are no Protestants—no consistent Protestants," he said. "Why, I am reading at this very time the proof of my statement."

"What is your proof, friend, that there are no true Protestants? That is a rather broad statement," said Mr. Anderson.

"Well, however broad it may sound, it is true. There are no consistent Protestants, for none of them take the Bible and the Bible only as their rule of faith. They say they follow the Bible; but in many things, they reject it altogether and follow the teachings and customs of the Catholic Church. For instance, you know very well that you have no Scripture for your Sunday—not a single word. The Bible teaches you that you should keep today, Saturday—not tomorrow. The Catholic Church, by authority of the apostle Peter, changed the day of worship from the seventh day to the first day of the week, and the whole religious world has adopted the change. And then to think that they persist in calling themselves Protestants! It is disgusting."

"But not all Protestants do as you say. There are exceptions."

"So far as I know, they all do. Of course, they grow indignant and make vigorous denial, but they do not dare come out and face the actual facts. Our church has challenged the whole Protestant world to show that they are not following its teachings rather than the Bible in their keeping of Sunday; but there has never been an answer. The reason is, there is no answer to be given.

Every intelligent Protestant clergyman who has studied church history knows that Sunday worship springs from our church. And so we say that, taking a part of our religion, they ought consistently to take it all. In fact, we look for all of you to come back into the true fold.

"A number of years ago," he continued, "one of our priests offered a thousand dollars to anyone who would bring even one text from the Bible to show Sunday to be the divine day of rest. But no one has ever appeared to claim the reward."

"No," said Mr. Anderson, "and no one ever will. Such a text cannot be found."

"Then why do you go on fooling yourself and others by keeping Sunday?"

"I do not," was the reply.

"Oh, you don't keep any day, I suppose."

"Yes, I observe the seventh day of the week. I am a Seventh-day Adventist. Now let me make you a proposition: Will you offer a reward of a thousand dollars to anyone who will prove from the Bible that your church did change the Sabbath?"

The man closed the catechism in his hand, looked Mr. Anderson squarely in the eye, and asked: "Who are you, anyway? What do you mean?"

"I mean," said the pastor, "that I agree with you that your church changed the Sabbath and that I am ready to show you, from the word of God, that you are correct."

"All right, provided you will use my Bible. And I will give you a hundred dollars if you make good your claims. It will be worth that much to me in handling the next Sunday man I meet. But remember, it must be from our Douay Version."

Mr. Anderson readily agreed; and the man, who had now introduced himself as James Conan, went after his

Bible, leaving his catechism lying in the deck chair.

"What have you here, brother?" asked Judge Kershaw, who happened along while Mr. Anderson was waiting; and stooping, he picked up the little book and opened it.

"A Catholic catechism! Well, this is strange literature for a Protestant pastor!"

The book had opened to the chapter devoted to church authority, and the judge's eye fell on these words: "*Q. Have you any other way of proving that the Church has power to institute festivals of precept? A.* Had she not such power, she could not have done that in which all modern religionists agree with her;—she could not have substituted the observance of Sunday the first day of the week, for the observance of Saturday the seventh day, a change for which there is no Scriptural authority."

Evidently the judge had never before read the statement, and he appeared greatly surprised; but an explanation was impossible, as Mr. Conan now returned. Handing Mr. Anderson the Bible, Mr. Conan renewed his conversation.

"Mr. Conan, you believe and receive the entire Bible, do you not?" was Mr. Anderson's first question.

"Yes, sir; every good Catholic does."

"I knew you must; for in the footnote that I find here in 2 Peter, I read: 'Every part of the Holy Scriptures was written by men inspired by the Holy Ghost, and declared as such by the church.' "

"Of course, Mr. Anderson, my belief is subject to the teaching of the church," Mr. Conan added.

"Well, let us note what the Bible says.

"In the book of Daniel, chapter 7, we are told of a vision given the prophet, a vision which revealed to him four great beasts—a lion, a bear, a leopard, and a beast without name. The footnote says, 'The Chaldean, Persian, Grecian and Roman empires.' Of the correctness of this position there is no doubt.

"In the vision, the prophet saw 'ten horns' on the fourth beast, and the footnote reads, *'Ten horns.* That is, ten kingdoms, . . . among which the empire of the fourth beast shall be parceled.' This too, without question, is correct; for between A.D. 351 and A.D. 476, the Western Empire was divided into exactly ten parts,—Franks, Alamanni, Burgundians, Suevi, Vandals, Visigoths, Anglo-Saxons, Lombards, Ostrogoths, and Heruli.

"After the ten horns (or kingdoms) appeared, the prophet said, 'another little horn sprung out of the midst of them: and three of the first horns were plucked up at the presence thereof. And behold eyes like the eyes of a man were in this horn, and a mouth speaking great things.' Between A.D. 493 and A.D. 538, exactly three of the horns (or kings) mentioned were plucked up, according to the prophecy. They were the Heruli, in Italy; the Vandals, in Africa; and the Ostrogoths, in Rome."

"I am familiar with that history," remarked Mr. Conan; "and you may be aware that they were overthrown because of their heretical positions, especially the Ostrogoths. The bishop of Rome was the one person who negotiated with the Eastern Empire for the cleansing of the Eternal City."

"Yes, you are right, Mr. Conan; it was a religious controversy that brought about the downfall of those three kingdoms. They were Arian in faith, and the church had them annihilated," said Mr. Anderson.

"But now mark: The horn that put them down had 'a mouth speaking great things.' Verse 8. In verse 24, this same horn is said to 'bring down three kings;' and then the prophet adds, 'And he shall think himself able to

change times and laws: and they shall be delivered into
his hand until a time and times and half a time.'

"I may not take time now to go largely into details,
but will call your attention to the last feature of the
description—that of the time. A 'time' is a year, even as
the footnote here states. In this prophecy, it is a prophetic year, equal to 360 prophetic days. According to
Ezekiel 4:6, a prophetic day equals a literal year. The
text reads, 'A day for a year, yea, a day for a year, I
have appointed to thee.' I have then the following:

Time	360 years
Times	720 years
Half a time	180 years
Total	1,260 years

"In Revelation 12:6, 14, this same period is clearly
shown to be one thousand two hundred sixty days, or
years; while in Revelation 13:5, it is stated to be 'forty and
two months' (thirty days to the Jewish month), which
gives the same number."

Mr. Conan apparently approved, as he was logically
obliged to do, the points thus far made, though it was
clear he was beginning to see what must be to him an
unwelcome conclusion.

"Twelve hundred sixty years is the time during which
this little horn would 'speak words,' 'crush the saints,'
and 'think himself able to change times and laws.' What
are the facts of history?

"In A.D. 533, Justinian, emperor of Eastern Rome,
issued a decree declaring the bishop of Rome the cor-
rector of heretics and 'head over all the churches.'
Immediately the work of putting down Arianism was
begun with new vengeance, in order that the decree

might become effective. The next year the Vandals were subjugated, this work being followed in 538 by the uprooting of the Ostrogoths. In A.D. 538, therefore, the bishop of Rome found himself the undisputed head of the great spiritual world, by royal decree, and from that date began his work outlined in the prophecy.

"Dating forward 1,260 years from A.D. 538, we are brought down to A.D. 1798. Was that a remarkable year in the history of the church of which the bishop of Rome was head? Ah, that was the time when the army of France took the head of the church prisoner, broke the power he had so long wielded, and carried him into captivity. The prophecy of Daniel was fulfilled almost to a day."

"Mr. Anderson," Mr. Conan said rather excitedly, "you are trying to prove the Catholic Church to be Antichrist. This is the worst thing I ever heard."

"Pardon me, Mr. Conan; but have I not taken it all from your Bible, as you suggested?"

"Well, pass it for the present. What about the Sabbath change? You have not proved anything yet as to the matter with which we began."

"Very good, let us proceed," said Mr. Anderson.

"The prophecy definitely states that this little horn should 'think himself able to change times and laws.' What laws are pointed out? Read the whole verse and see. The horn is working against God—against God's name, against God's people, and against God's laws. And right here let me ask you a question: Does not your literature teach that the pope, speaking *ex cathedra,* has authority to set aside the words of Scripture for the good of the church?"

"I must acknowledge that it does."

"Does not your catechism, which you have in your

hand, actually set before you a changed form of the law of God?"

"I do not know," Mr. Conan replied.

Taking the catechism proffered, Mr. Anderson turned to the chapter devoted to the commandments, and read, at the same time comparing with Mr. Conan's Bible.

"Now, Mr. Conan, notice. The fourth command is changed in your catechism, and calls for Sunday instead of Sabbath worship. And right over here the change is cited as proof that the church has authority to appoint other special days of service. In other words, your church actually confesses to changing the word of God. As you told me at the beginning, she changed the day."

Judge Kershaw had been only an interested listener. But now he spoke, saying: "Mr. Anderson has given evidence which would be accepted in any court of law. It is a case in which the defendant has been proved guilty not only by direct testimony of unimpeachable witnesses, but by his own confession as well."

"Mr. Conan, these are hard things; but let me go a step further," continued Mr. Anderson. "The Church of Rome has fulfilled another great prophecy, that of 2 Thessalonians 2:3, 4, which speaks of 'the man of sin, . . . the son of perdition, . . . who opposeth and is lifted up above all that is called God or that is worshiped, so that he sitteth in the temple [the church] of God, showing himself as if he were God.' The pope has put himself above God in setting aside a portion of His law; he has assumed titles that belong to God only; he has allowed himself, as Christ's pretended vicar, to receive worship and adoration; and all this has been in the temple—the church—of God. Is it not true, then, that the Church of Rome is the power that fulfills Daniel 7:25 and that changed the Sabbath of Jehovah?"

"Mr. Anderson, this is terrible. Do the priests know these things?"

"Yes, my brother, many of them do; and not only the priests, but Protestant ministers as well." He then read Ezekiel 22:26.

Mr. Conan seemed stunned, but in no wise resentful. He was on a mission for the church. What should he now do about it?

CHAPTER XV

A Choice That Is Vital

MR. ANDERSON had no sooner reached his stateroom than a messenger boy called with a note and said that he had been asked to wait for a reply.

The note was from Mrs. Slocum, one of the women from San Francisco, who had been so impressed by the pastor's prayer during the service of the previous Tuesday. It read as follows:

"MY DEAR MR. ANDERSON:

"For several days there has been developing an increasing desire on the part of many of the passengers to hear from you concerning the question of the Sabbath. The matter seems to us of such importance that we wish to press you once more into service. Will you address us tomorrow (Sunday) in the parlor, of course choosing such phases of the subject as you may deem best? Kindly reply by messenger.

"(MRS.) FRANCES SLOCUM."

In justice to Mr. Anderson, it must be said he was not one who sought opportunity to minister propaganda, nor did he believe in that most unfortunate practice termed proselyting. His was a mission of true soul winning. But one purpose actuated him; namely, to preach Christ and Him crucified. He believed thoroughly, however, in the necessity of teaching doctrine; for without that, there would be no guide to conduct, no track over which the believer could successfully direct his train of life to the kingdom of God.

This invitation revealed to him real heart hunger, or, changing the figure, soil that was ready for the sowing of the seed. He therefore penned a short note of acceptance, and began to give thought to what he should say.

Little did he know that God had ordained the service to be one of the most momentous in his life.

The hour came, and the parlor was filled. Dr. Spaulding and Mr. and Mrs. Gregory sat in the front, their faces beaming with anticipation. Judge Kershaw occupied a commanding position, while nearby were Mr. Severance and Harold Wilson with his Bible in his hand. Of course, Mrs. Slocum and her friends were where they could see and hear all; and, strangely enough, Mr. Conan was in the audience.

How different was the atmosphere of this service from that of a few days before! Within so brief a space of time, the grace of God had wrought mightily on hearts, yet working through the humblest of agencies. Today there was freedom in the lives of both ministers and people, which had never before been known, because never before had they yielded to the truth, which makes and keeps free. John 8:32, 36.

To the utter astonishment of a large number present, Captain Mann opened the meeting by prayer—a prayer such as that parlor had never heard before and perhaps would not hear again.

"O God in heaven," he began with trembling tone, "we indeed thank Thee at this hour that Thou hast called us to Thy side. We thank Thee for Thy goodness which has followed us all through our lives. We thank Thee for our beautiful mothers, who, while we were children, sought under Thy direction to cause our feet to walk the paths of righteousness, who taught us to pray, who taught us to love and obey Thy commandments. And surely Thou art better than mothers, for Thou madest them and gavest them to us. We can and do trust Thee. We want today to have Thee take us and hold us in Thy great, strong arms. We are tired of the world and its folly. Take us, therefore, Saviour, and give us rest, as Thou hast promised. We yield to Thy Spirit. Now teach us. Guide us into the very fullness of truth. Thou art guiding, and we are following. However unwilling we may have been, we are not unwilling today. And, Blessed One, search through this company, and help, greatly help, all who are longing for perfect victory. There are some here who are learning new things, which may be hard to receive; but help them learn. Bring us fully out of the darkness of all erroneous belief, and give us courage to do the right no matter what the cost, that one day, at the journey's end, we may see our mothers again, and see Thee in glory. Grant it all because of Thy promise and because of our great need. Through the merits of Jesus, Thy Son and our Saviour, we ask it. Amen."

There were frequent amens; and as the captain arose from his knees—for he had knelt to pray—more than one handkerchief was used to dry eyes that had been moistened by tender memories of early days.

Mr. Anderson arose and was about to speak; but ere he could do so, Mrs. Slocum spoke.

"Pastor," she said, "are you willing to use the marked Bible on this occasion? Somehow the prayer has caused me to regard this meeting as a kind of mothers' meeting, and this Bible is surely a mother's Bible. This is only a bit of sentiment, it is true; yet it will prove a blessing to some."

Harold Wilson gladly brought forward the Bible and placed it on the speaker's stand. Thus a mother's voice continued to speak, a mother's prayer continued to be answered. How truly do one's works follow when God is permitted to have His way in the life!

"My friends," said Mr. Anderson, "as you probably know, I am speaking today by request. There are those who are eager to know more fully of the truth of the gospel as revealed in the Sabbath of the Lord; and to help such, I will briefly set before you a few principles not before noticed. I can do no better, I think, than to answer a question that was handed in by someone last Tuesday. The question reads, 'What do you understand by the mark of the beast in Revelation 13:17?'

"Without doubt, I must be brief; so you will gladly allow me the privilege of omitting the usual sermon style of phraseology and of treating you as a class of students, who may interrupt with questions as you desire.

"I will first call your attention to the fact that 'the beast' of Revelation 12, 13, and 17 is earthly power, earthly government, under the influence of Satan and controlled by the church, standing in opposition to God. It is, so far as Revelation 13 is concerned, the power of earthly government swayed by the papal church, which for 'forty and two months' of prophetic time (1,260 literal years, reaching from A.D. 538 to A.D. 1798) spoke 'great things and blasphemies,' and to whom 'it was given . . . to make war with the saints, and to overcome them.' See verses 5-7. It was that terrible system known as 'that man of sin, . . . the son of perdition,' which took its place in the church of God, secured control of the Roman Empire, put tradition in the place of the Bible, and actually changed God's law, substituting Sunday for the Sabbath. See 2 Thessalonians 2:3, 4; Daniel 7:25. All these things are matters of history and may be read by all.

"You will see at a glance, therefore, that 'the mark of the beast' must be something intimately associated with the papacy in its work of opposing God's truth and people; for Revelation 14:9-11 distinctly states that to receive this mark puts one into direct warfare against God and makes him a subject of wrath. The mark, then, is a terribly serious proposition; and surely inspiration must make plain to us what it is.

"So far as the mere word is concerned, 'mark' is equivalent to 'seal' or 'sign.' The words are used interchangeably. For instance, in Ezekiel 9:4, God tells the heavenly messenger to 'set a *mark upon the foreheads*' of the men who honor Him; while in Revelation 7:3 we find these same people '*sealed . . . in their foreheads.*' In Romans 4:11, the words 'sign' and 'seal' stand as equivalents: 'He received the sign of circumcision, a seal of the righteousness of the faith which he had.' It would be perfectly proper, therefore, to speak of the mark of God; for one would be well understood as meaning the seal of God, or, if you please, the *sign* of God.

"To put the matter as it really is, the beast has its mark, its sign, its seal; and opposed are God's mark, God's sign, God's seal. To have the mark, or sign, or seal of the beast is to die; to have the mark, or sign, or seal of God is to live, and to live forever.

"But now we come to the really interesting part of the matter. These terms—'mark,' 'sign,' 'seal'—are used in the word of God with special reference to law, or legal documents. Jezebel 'wrote letters in Ahab's name, and sealed them with his seal.' 1 Kings 21:8. The decree of Haman for the destruction of the Jews in the days of Esther was 'in the name of King Ahasuerus, . . . and sealed with the king's ring.' Esther 3:12. This was the thought of the signet ring—the name ring—of the ancient times. The king's name was in the ring; and the impress of the ring was to stamp the king's name. In this way, documents were sealed, and thus became law. We have only to remember this to see the point we are after: God's seal, or sign, is something connected with His law. It is the signet portion, that in which His name is found, and therefore that which gives it the force of true law.

"I need not remind you that three essential features are to be found in every law seal: first, the name of the official; second, his designated office; and third, the territory over which his authority extends. Thus the President of our country, in signing any bill or other document, must sign his name, with the title appended, 'President of the United States.' It is not enough that he sign only his name, for there might be other persons of the same name. Nor is it sufficient that he give only his name and office; for a person bearing his name might be president of a transit company or a literary club. No; it takes all three: 1, the name; 2, 'President' (office); and 3, 'United States of America' (territory).

"Let me now inquire if this principle is really recognized in God's law, the Ten Commandments.

"The first and the last five of the commandments do not mention Jehovah's name, so we will pass them. The second, the third, and the fifth give only His name. But the fourth, the Sabbath command, brings to view His name, His office, His realm. 'The seventh day is the

Sabbath of the Lord [Jehovah] thy God'—here is His name. 'In six days the Lord made heaven and earth, the sea, and all that in them is'—here He gives His office as Creator and the extent of His authority as heaven and earth. Jehovah, Creator of the universe—this is His official seal. The fourth commandment is the official seal of the divine law; and without it, that law would be invalid. Do you all see that this is so?'"

There was no question. The truth was self-evident.

"God Himself constantly points to the fact that He is Creator of all things, as reason why we should obey. See Genesis 1:1; Exodus 20:8-11; Jeremiah 10:10-12; Psalms 96:5; 33:6-9; and other texts. And if any of you are going abroad as missionaries to the heathen, remember that only the truth of the fourth commandment, coupled with a conscientious observance of it, will convince them of the supremacy of our God."

"Kindly explain that a little further," said Dr. Spaulding.

"Well, while the heathen believes in the greatness of his god or gods, he does not worship them as having creative power. Thus when you come to him with authoritative word that Jehovah is the Creator, that He therefore made all the things which the heathen has worshiped, he sees that even the gods themselves must bow to Jehovah's commands. The Sabbath command thus becomes the signal for him to transfer his allegiance; and *your obedience helps him* to understand that God still lives and re-creates those who yield to Him."

"That is fine, brother, fine," said Dr. Spaulding. "We missionaries may well take the lesson to heart."

Now Mr. Conan spoke. "Mr. Anderson," he said, "what about the mark of the beast? You are not touching that point."

"I think, Mr. Conan," said the minister, "I will let you answer your own question. If the Sabbath commandment is the seal of God (and it is), and if the mark, or seal, of the beast stands in opposition to it, then, logically, what must we conclude as to the character of the mark?"

"Why, logically, I should say it also is a Sabbath of some kind—that is, Sabbath opposing Sabbath," was Mr. Conan's reply.

"Exactly so," said Mr. Anderson, "and that is a historical fact, as I showed you yesterday. The beast, the papacy, a combination of church and state, in the fourth century of our era, succeeded in substituting tradition for the word of God, and, wickedly attacking the truth of the fourth commandment, substituted Sunday for the Sabbath. Eusebius, a bishop of that period, openly claimed that 'all things whatsoever that it was duty to do on the Sabbath these *we* have transferred to the Lord's day.' And not very long ago, one of the leading Catholic papers of the United States made the statement that 'the Catholic Church of its own infallible authority created Sunday as a holy day to take the place of the Sabbath of the old law.' 'We observe Sunday instead of Saturday,' says a catechism that I saw yesterday, 'because the Catholic Church, in the Council of Laodicea (A.D. 336), transferred the solemnity from Saturday to Sunday.'

"Now, as God points to His Sabbath seal as evidence of His authority, so the Church of Rome points to her Sunday mark as evidence of her authority. She proves her right to command feasts and holy days 'by the very act' (this from a catechism) 'of changing the Sabbath into Sunday.' Thus her 'mark' is set in boastful opposition to God's 'seal.'

"Summing all up, we have this: An apostate power has violated God's law by tearing out its seal and putting

Sunday in its place. Then apostasy comes to men and demands of them that they accept the change it has made, enforcing its claims by law wherever and whenever it has sufficient influence to do so. All the Sunday laws of our own and other lands have this wretched principle behind them. And lest some of you do not know, I may say here that both the prophecies of God's word and the plans of the present Roman Church show that erelong all nations will pass laws making Sunday observance universal, and finally compelling men to keep it or die. Read all of Revelation 13.

"Many Christians have observed the Sunday in good conscience, believing they were doing the will of God; and He accepted the motive, the heart love. But now light is shining. God warns us against that apostate system comprised in the beast and his image, which exalts the false sabbath in the place of the true, and seeks to enforce it under penalties. Thus it becomes its mark. *And when men in the light of God's message reject God's day, and accept as their badge of allegiance the Sunday as enforced by the beast and his image, they receive the mark of the beast,* against which God warns. At what stage in men's experience men cut themselves off from God, it is not for mortals to say. Judgment rests with God.

"At this time, therefore, God is calling upon us to turn again to His law and keep it wholly. He pleads with us to restore the Sabbath to its place. See Isaiah 8:16. He counsels us to tread it underfoot no longer. Isaiah 58:13. He commands His messengers to stay the tide of human conflict until we have received its truth into our lives. Revelation 7:1-3. He sends to the whole world a great gospel message inviting men to worship Him only— Him who created all things. Revelation 14:6, 7. And finally He shows us that many will refuse to receive the

Sunday mark, but, taking God fully into their lives, will keep all His commandments (Revelation 14:12), and, sealed with His seal, stand at last upon Mount Zion in the kingdom of glory. Revelation 14:1. On the other hand, those who reject God's message, who swing off with the world to please that power which opposes God, and thus partake of the spirit and character of the world, will drink the wine of His wrath (Revelation 14:9-11), and suffer the awfulness of those plagues which will then depopulate the earth. Revelation 16.

"Do you wonder, my friends, that I am interested in this matter? Is it worth your while to study it? Will any here today even think of treating the question lightly? Which will it be with you—Rome or Christ, the Sunday or the Sabbath, the mark of the beast or the seal of the living God?"

Dr. Spaulding almost leaped to his feet. "Mr. Anderson," he said, "may I be permitted a few words?"

As he faced the people, it was evident that he had something to say which was to mark a new era in his own life, and which would profoundly affect the lives of many others.

CHAPTER XVI

The Fruitage of the Marked Bible

DR. SPAULDING seemed unable to get his voice. A picture of his whole past life rose before him, and a sense of his great unworthiness seemed almost to overwhelm him.

"My dear people," he began, "without doubt, you are all aware that during this journey I have been making a most determined effort to combat, in every way I could, the thought that the fourth commandment should be observed by Christians.

"I have even wished, since this journey began, that something would occur to silence the voice of this young man, Mr. Wilson. I really have hated him and his Bible as well.

"But God has opened my eyes. He has touched my heart and softened it. He has fulfilled the new-covenant promise, and today I can truly say that I delight to do His will. The law that I wanted to think was abolished, and the Sabbath that I despised and even abhorred, are now written in my mind, and I am resting in Him.

"Mr. Wilson had a godly mother. She loved God's word. She wanted her boy to love it. And to that end she put her tears and her prayers into this Volume [here he took the marked Bible from the stand], trusting that in some way, her work of love would be blessed in heaven. That it has been, you can all see. Her son has found the Lord. But let me tell you, dear ones, this Book and his mother's prayers have been the means also of arresting me in my headstrong course."

So earnest, so sincere, so tender, was his testimony, that the very air seemed filled with the love of God.

"And are you really going with me, Dr. Spaulding?" asked Harold Wilson.

Dr. Spaulding responded by opening a folded paper that he held in his hand. It was his letter of resignation to the board under whose auspices he had started out on his mission. He then read:

"DEAR BRETHREN:

"This is to inform you that God has miraculously wrought upon my life, and has brought me to understand that for years, like Saul of Tarsus, I have been foolishly kicking against the pricks. Even before the completion of my journey across the sea, I find myself so entirely at variance with my former belief and teaching, that I am obliged to desist from the purpose which sent me to the Orient and to ask you to accept my resignation as a member of the Board of Foreign Missions.

"That you may understand me fully, kindly allow me a brief statement concerning past personal experiences.

"As you well know, I have been frequently chosen by my brethren to enter the arena of debate, to defend our views against the supposedly erroneous doctrines of the Sabbatarians. I have been regarded as eminently successful in my efforts. It was I, also, who was selected a few years ago to conduct the campaign against the violators of our Arkansas State Sunday law. And here, too, I was regarded as successful; for I secured several convictions and had a vote of commendation from our district conference.

"But throughout my ministry, there has followed me constantly a strange though somewhat vague consciousness that my views were not well founded in Scripture. Many a time, even while in the heat of argument, I have heard a voice telling me I was wrong; but I refused to listen, thinking it only a foolish and temporary weakness of my own nature. The thought of halting and of testing my views was also steadfastly put aside, for the reason that I feared change, and besides, my pride and my love of my people's approval outweighed my love of truth.

"There has come to me, however, a series of providences which has brought me to my knees. The door of life has been swung so wide open, the light of inspiration has shone so clearly, and the love of God has so led me to repentance, that I have fully surrendered my heart to the influences of the Holy Spirit. I have found the actual way of life; and following Jesus Christ, I am glad in Him. My questions and doubts are gone, and the Spirit bears witness that I have been born again.

"In a word, dear brethren, I am now a Sabbathkeeper, an observer of the seventh day.

"Begging your indulgence a little further, I take the privilege of giving you a few of the principal reasons, gathered from the Bible, for my present course of action.

"1. God's word in its entirety is authoritatively from Him. 2 Timothy 3:16, 17; Romans 15:4.

"2. Jesus Christ was the Author. 2 Peter 2:21; 1 Peter 1:10, 11.

"3. The Old Testament, as well as the New, reveals Christ. Luke 24:25-27; John 5:39.

"4. The gospel was known, and by it men were saved through faith, from the very beginning. Revelation 13:8; Galatians 3:8; with John 8:56; Hebrews 4:1, 2.

"5. The gospel saves from sin (Matthew 1:21; Romans 1:16); sin is the transgression of the moral law (1 John 3:4); and the law points out the sin from which the gospel saves (Romans 3:20).

"6. Sin entered the world at the beginning (Romans 5:12), and sin is not imputed where there is no law (Romans 4:16; 5:13). Therefore the law dates from the foundation of the world.

"7. The Sabbath, as a part of God's law, was given to our first parents. Genesis 2:1-3.

"8. It was made for the whole race of mankind. Mark 2:27.

"9. As Christ was the Creator (John 1:1-3, 14; Colossians 1:13-16), even so it was He who made the Sabbath and gave it to man. The Sabbath of the law is the Sabbath of Christ.

"10. And Christ Himself, the Mediator, gave the law on Sinai. Galatians 3:19 with 1 Timothy 2:5. The Ten Commandments are specially the gift of Jesus Christ.

"11. As we have seen, Christ spoke through the prophets. 1 Peter 1:10, 11. And through the prophets, He foretold His love for the law. Psalm 40:7, 8; Isaiah 42:21.

"12. When He came into the world, He lived and taught the sacred and far-reaching claims of the Ten Commandments. John 15:10; Matthew 5:17, 18; 19:17.

"13. The New Testament throughout follows Jesus' teaching, and proclaims the authority of the law. Romans 3:31; James 2:8-12; Revelation 22:14.

"14. There has been absolutely no change in that law since it was given in Eden, for God is unchangeable. Malachi 3:6; Psalm 89:34; Matthew 5:18.

"15. The Sabbath, placed in the very bosom of the law, and a vital part of its great moral nature, has come to us, therefore, unchanged and unchangeable.

"16. All through the ages, the Sabbath has been made the test of obedience, the sign of loyalty. Exodus 16:4, 27, 28; Jeremiah 17:24, 25; Exodus 31:16, 17; Ezekiel 20: 12, 20.

"17. As the seal of God's law, it is the great gospel test of the last days of time. Revelation 7:1-3; 14:6, 7. Compare Isaiah 56:1-8.

"18. The cycle of the week has come down to us without confusion or loss of count from Paradise, as is shown by the records of all nations, ancient and modern, which have agreed often even in the names of the days.

"19. From the time of Sinai, the Jewish nation has sacredly preserved the seventh day; and Sinai pointed out and identified the seventh day of creation. Without doubt, therefore, our week and its seventh day are identical with the week at the beginning.

"20. Jesus kept the Sabbath (Luke 4:16), and therefore I should.

"21. The women who were most associated with Christ kept it after the crucifixion. Luke 23:56.

"22. The apostles observed it. Acts 17:2; 18:4, etc.

"23. The seventh day was observed by the Christian church generally for more than two centuries after Christ.

"24. Sunday was the great day of ancient pagan sun worship; and the custom of meeting on that day was introduced by ambitious, worldly churchmen to please the tastes of the multitudes and to make Christianity popular. Had the church been faithful, Sunday observance would never have been known.

"25. In the fourth century, when the church was completely fallen, she joined hands with the state; and thus Sunday became established by law and has continued until now. The Church of Rome changed the Sabbath, according to the prophecy of Daniel 7:25.

"26. But though the Sabbath has been set aside by the world at large, God is now calling upon men to honor Him by its observance (Isaiah 58:13), and warns them against following the papacy and receiving its mark (Revelation 14:9-11).

"27. Some will heed His message and keep *all* His commandments. Revelation 14:12.

"28. These will be sealed with His name and, in the better world, continue eternally to enjoy the blessed rest of the Sabbath, which they found in Christ here. Revelation 14:1; Isaiah 66:22, 23.

"Now, brethren, in view of all these passages, I have fully given my heart to God in new covenant relationship, and am already finding blessing in the gift of His holy Sabbath. And so beautiful is this new life, that I cannot bid you farewell without inviting you to go with me. Will you not join me in the fullest possible consecration, and thus find that power which will enable us speedily to evangelize the world and bring the glad day of final victory?

"Your brother and co-worker,

"HUGH M. SPAULDING."

"Yes, Harold, I am going with you. This day I offer my service to my Master as a true missionary of the cross; and if my Sabbathkeeping brethren shall find my gift acceptable, I shall experience great joy in taking my place among them in their work of preparing a people for the great day of God.

"And now, in closing, may I ask if others here are not ready to join me?"

The effect of the confession and invitation was electric. Almost a score of persons quickly stood.

Judge Kershaw caught Dr. Spaulding's hand.

"Friends," said he, "this day and its remarkable blessings lead me to say, as Simeon said in the temple, 'Lord, now lettest Thou Thy servant depart in peace, according to Thy word: for mine eyes have seen Thy salvation.' I have found rest, and for the first time in my nearly seventy years, I have peace."

Then Mr. Severance turned, and, facing the passengers, he said: "I have been a man of business for more than thirty years. From a child, I have always wanted to be right; but somehow I had come to believe that Christianity had little in it, and that so far as I was concerned, there was nothing better to do than to live a clean life and trust to come out all right in the end.

"To please my wife, and possibly to help my business, I joined the church a few years ago; but it has been nothing to me except a form, and really I have been unhappy in my heart.

"Two years ago I heard Mr. Anderson preach in San Francisco. His words were plain; and in a way, his message appealed to me—however, only intellectually. My heart was not touched.

"But last Tuesday, God brought home to me, in Mr. Anderson's words, a conviction of my sin and a vision of what He wished me to be. I saw in his Sabbath message a light that showed me my true character. My sin rose before me, and I was overwhelmed with condemnation. Yet in it all, there was comfort. The Spirit has healed. Today I am a new man, by the grace of God, and the Sabbath is my delight. I know now what it is to be a man—an honest man after God's order."

"This delightful testimony from Mr. Severance," said Mr. Anderson, "leads me to offer a word further, a word of confession. The reason my preaching of a few years ago appealed only to my brother's intellectuality was that I had not yet found the secret of preaching Christ and Him crucified. My evangelistic work was largely formal and therefore did not truly reach hearts. I thank the Lord that I have found the better way."

At this point, to the surprise of many, Mr. Conan rose from his seat, and said: "Friends, I was born and reared in the Roman Catholic Church and have always boasted that nothing could ever influence me to change my faith. My church was to me the only church. Until only a little more than twenty hours ago, I never found anything to cause me the least anxiety about my faith. But here I am, at this hour, completely changed. My hands are no longer bound by the shackles of priest or pope. I am in a new world of truth, of beauty, of freedom. I have found Jesus Christ; and with all my heart, I expect to serve Him. I want to ask the prayers of Mr. Anderson, through whom my revelation and deliverance have come. I, too, like Dr. Spaulding, was on a mission for my church; but I abandon it all, that I may join with true Protestants in delivering men from the errors of the time, and particularly from the mark of apostasy."

"Isn't this marvelous!" exclaimed Mrs. Slocum, in a voice that could be heard throughout the room. "This is what I have long waited to see. I want everyone to know that I am a Sabbathkeeper from this day forward."

Captain Mann, standing with others, now found opportunity to add his word. "After fifty years of much blindness," he began, "my eyes have finally been opened. I thought I knew what I did not know. I was certain, for one thing, that Jesus Christ changed the Sabbath to Sunday, and that on this account I was under obligation to observe the first day for His sake. But my investigation has shown me that only ignorance can accept that position. Christ didn't change the day, but the papacy did.

As a Protestant, therefore, and as one who believes fully in the everlasting claims of the law of God, and who takes the Bible and the Bible only as the rule of faith and practice, I give my hand and heart, my life and time and all, to the blessed truth which I have found. Hereafter the world shall know me as a Seventh-day Adventist. God helping me, I can do naught else. This is my last trans-pacific journey as captain."

Mr. and Mrs. Gregory next bore their testimony of surrender to God's commands, Mrs. Gregory speaking particularly of her deliverance from the sea by the hand of one whom she had despised and hated.

That day, seventeen persons joined hands to serve God in the fullness of a new-found love and a new gift of power. The marked Bible had wrought its work. A mother's prayers had been more than answered.

Several years have since passed, but the good work has gone steadily forward. Harold Wilson returned to San Francisco, and, aided by Mr. Severance, perfected his education, entered the ministry, and now, as an ordained minister, is doing a mighty work in a foreign land. Captain Mann established a home for sailors, and Harold's marked Bible was made a strong feature in its work of soul saving. Many a young man has found a heart awakening through contact with the Book and through hearing the story of the mother who gave it.

Dr. Spaulding and Mr. Gregory, true to their convictions, are continuing their ministry in two of our Eastern cities. Splendid indeed has been their success in leading sinners to "the Lamb of God, which taketh away the sin of the world." Dr. Spaulding's written statement of resignation led some of his former co-workers to follow him in the path of fuller light. Mr. Conan is now manager of

a large religious institution, and, withal, is a deeply spiritual man of God. With him, religion and business are
identical.

How wonderful are our Father's providences! Let us
learn the lesson that His word cannot fail and that a
mother's prayers will surely be answered.